TAKE OFF YOUR SHOES

D1557769

MARK LINK, S.J.

by ARGUS COMMUNICATIONS

A Division of DLM, Inc.
7440 Natchez Avenue • Niles, Illinois 60648 U.S.A.

ernational Standard Book Number: 0-913592-05-6

and it
was good

CONTENTS

ACKNOWLEDGEMENTS

Vanguard Press, Inc. for *Studs Lonigan* by James T. Farrell.

Alfred A. Knopf, Inc. for *God and My Father* by Clarence Day.

Alfred A. Knopf, Inc. for *The Stranger* by Albert Camus.

Look Magazine (Feb. 6, 1968) for "A Visit With India's High-Powered New Prophet" by Paul Horn.

Random House, Inc. for "Man of La Mancha," lyrics by Joe Darion.

"Testimony of a 20th Century Catholic" by Morris West reprinted with permission from *America*, Dec. 2, 1967. All rights reserved. © 1967. America Press, Inc., 106 W. 56th Street, New York, New York 10019.

Sheed & Ward for *Theology and Sanity* by Frank Sheed.

"The Wind of Change" by Rod McKuen, copyright © 1971 by Montcalm Productions, Inc., from the book "Pastorale" published by Stanyan Books and Random House, Inc.

Holt, Rinehart & Winston, Inc. for *The Sane Society* by Erich Fromm.

Charles Scribner's Sons for *Of Flight and Life* by Charles Lindbergh.

Herder and Herder for *Prayers, Poems & Songs* by Huub Osterhuis.

G. Schirmer, Inc. for *Mass*, lyrics by Leonard Bernstein and Stephen Schwartz.

Catholic Digest (June, 1949) for "Why I Know There is a God" by Fulton Oursler.

Westminster Press for *Honest Religion for Secular Man* by Leslie Newbign.

Alfred A. Knopf, Inc. for *Markings* by Dag Hammarskjöld. Copyright © by Alfred A. Knopf, Inc.

Commonweal Magazine (Dec. 5, 1969) for "Defending Freedom, Preventing Bloodbaths" by Peter Steinfels.

Harper & Row, Inc. for *Strength to Love* by Martin Luther King.

Coward-McCann, Inc. for *Cain, Where is Your Brother* by Francois Mauriac.

Charles Scribner's Sons for *The Range of Reason* by Jacques Maritain.

Harper & Row, Inc. for *Kerygma and Myth* by Rudolf Bultmann.

J. Murray, Inc. for *Manfred* by Lord Byron.

G. Bell & Sons, Ltd. for *Table Talk* by Samuel Taylor Coleridge.

Sheed & Ward for *The End of Our Time* by Nicholas Berdyaev.

E. P. Dutton & Co., Inc. for *Pensées* by Blaise Pascal.

Random House, Inc. for *Nature* by Ralph Waldo Emerson.

J. M. Dent & Co. for *Lectures on the English Comic Writers* by William Hazlitt.

H. Holt & Co. for *On the Heights* by B. Auerbach.

Harper & Row, Inc. for *Moby Dick* by Herman Melville.

Harper & Row, Inc. for *The Social Gospel Reexamined* by F. Ernest Johnson.

Modern Library for *Varieties of Religious Experience* by William James.

W. W. Norton & Co., Inc. for *Faith and Freedom* by Barbara Ward.

Ahmedabad Navajivian Publishing House for *My Experiment with Truth* by Mohandus K. Gandhi.

Harcourt Brace Jovanovich, Inc. for *The Little Prince* by Antoine de Saint-Exupery.

Harcourt Brace Jovanovich, Inc. for *Growth Games* by Howard R. Lewis and Harold S. Streitfeld.

Life Magazine (Jan. 9, 1970) for "The Quest for Spiritual Survival."

W. W. Norton & Co., Inc. for *Man's Search for Himself* by Rollo May. Copyright © by W. W. Norton & Co., Inc.

Lumen Vitae (Vol. 25, No. 4, 1970) for "Incarnation" by Robrecht Michiels.

Doubleday & Co., Inc. for *The Gospels Without Myth* by Louis Evely. Copyright © by Doubleday & Co., Inc.

Herder and Herder for *Man Becoming* by Gregory Baum.

Westminster Press for *Honest to God* by John Robinson.

Homiletic and Pastoral Review (May 5, 1970) for an excerpt from "Finding God in the City" by Edward Echlin.

Herder and Herder for *God is With Us* by Ladislaus Boros.

Simon & Schuster, Inc. for "The Seventh Seal" from *Four Screenplays of Ingmar Bergman*.

Fawcett World Library for *Pigeon Feathers and Other Stories* by John Updike.

Viking Press, Inc. for *A Story Teller's Tale* by Sherwood Anderson.

Wm. Morrow & Co., Inc. for *The Devil's Advocate* by Morris West.

Sheed & Ward for *God and Man* by Edward Schillebeeckx.

James Connor, S. J. for permission to reprint from his lecture series "The Experience of God." Lectures originally delivered at Summer College for Spiritual Renewal, Loyola College, Baltimore.

Modern Library for *Apologia Pro Vita Sua* by John Henry Newman.

America Magazine (June 10, 1965) for "William James and Alcoholics Anonymous" by Robert Roth.

The Macmillan Co. for *Atheism in Our Time* by Ignace Lepp. Copyright © by the Macmillan Co.

Harper & Row, Inc. for *Stride Toward Freedom* by Martin Luther King. Copyright © by Harper & Row Publishers, Inc.

The Macmillan Co. for *A Search for God in Time and Memory* by John S. Dunne. Copyright © 1969 by John S. Dunne, C.S.C.

Today Magazine (March, 1968) for "The Restless Believers" by John J. Kirvan.

Concordia Publishing House for *I Hate to Bother You, But . . .* by William Hulme.

Nothing Fixed or Final copyright © 1969 by Sydney Carter. All rights reserved. Used by permission of Galaxy Music Corp., New York, sole U. S. agent.

The Catholic World (March, 1969) for "The Fabric of Modern Faith" by Vincent Rugiero.

Random House, Inc. for *Listen to the Warm* by Rod McKuen. Copyright © 1967 by Rod McKuen and Anita Kerr. Reprinted by permission of Random House, Inc.

T. J. Kenedy for *The Golden String* by Bede Griffith.

Regnery, Henry, Co. for *The Lord* by Romano Guardini.

Yale University Press for *The Courage to Be* by Paul Tillich.

Doubleday & Co., Inc. for *The Story of My Life* by Helen Keller. Copyright © by Doubleday & Co., Inc.

Paulist/Newman Press for *Faith and Doctrine* by Gregory Baum. Copyright © by Paulist/Newman Press.

Alfred A. Knopf for *The Prophet* by Kahlil Gibran.

U.S. Catholic/Jubilee (July, 1970) for "Are We Losing the Faith?" by Gregory Baum.

Harper & Row, Inc. for *Life on the Mississippi* by Mark Twain.

J. B. Lippincott Co. for *The Weekenders* by Max Gunther.

The Macmillan Co. for *Alice's Adventures in Wonderland* by Lewis Carroll.

Doubleday & Co., Inc. for *The Everlasting Man* by Gilbert K. Chesterton.

Random House, Inc. for *Gift From the Sea* by Anne Morrow Lindbergh. Copyright © by Vantage Books, a division of Random House, Inc.

Flemming H. Revell Co. for *Man Does Not Stand Alone* by A. Cressy Morrison.

DESIGN BY GENE TARPEY

PHOTO CREDITS

Joe Benge 41, 55, 60, 66B, 73, 86, 98, 114B
Paul Borgman 74
E. Butenas 67
Mike Deane 11T, 62B, 66T, 68B, 119B, 121
John Hasse 6, 32
David Hoffman 20, 49B, 51, 101, 112
Leon Isaza 30B, 45C, 46-47, 111, 116-117
Bob Johnson 10, 65, 69, 82, 97, 99
Algimantas Kezys 52
Mike Kipley Cover, 9, 81R
Robert Kopek 45T
Gene Korba 21, 28, 33B, 44C, 64, 85, 96

Chuck Lieberman 8, 14-15, 22, 24B, 25B, 26, 31, 36, 42, 43, 44T, 54, 78, 87, 90, 91, 94, 95, 115
Sr. Mary Lucas 106
Bob McKendrick 38, 48, 58, 62T, 72, 92, 100, 107, 118-119
Patrick H. O'Leary 110
David Rolston 68T
Wm. Siegrist 109
Gerry Souter 5
Gene Tarpey 11B, 12, 13, 17, 18, 24T, 27, 29, 33T, 34, 35, 40, 49T, 56, 70, 76, 77, 79, 80B, 84, 88, 89, 104, 105, 108T
James Vorwoldt 19B, 30T, 45B, 80T, 108B, 114T
W. M. Wolff 16, 61, 113

I

PARADOX

man alone

WHERE IS HE?

I'd like to see God.
I'd like to tell him a few things.
I'd like to say,
"God, why do you create men
and make them suffer and fight in vain,
and live brief unhappy lives like pigs,
and make them die disgustingly,
and rot?

God, why do
the beautiful girls you create
become whores, grow old and toothless,
die and have their corpses rot
so that they are a stench
to human nostrils?

God, why do you permit
thousands and millions of your creatures,
made in your image and likeness,
to live like crowded dogs
in slums and tenements,
while an exploiting few
profit from the sweat of their toil,
produce nothing,
and live in kingly mansions?

God, why do you permit men
to starve, hunger, die from syphilis,
cancer, consumption?
God, why do you not raise
one little finger to save man
from all the . . . suffering
on this human planet?"

That's what I'd say to God
if I could find him hiding behind a tree.
But God is a wise guy.
He keeps in hiding.

James T. Farrell
Studs Lonigan

BAD SCENE

I turned to speak
    to God
About the world's despair;
But to make
    matters worse,
I found
    God wasn't there.

Robert Frost
"Not All There"

COP OUT?

It is easier for me
to think of a world
without a creator

than of a creator loaded with
all the contradictions
of the world.

Simone de Beauvoir

BLIND TRUST

. . . even though the fig
does not blossom,
nor fruit grow on the vine,
even though . . .
fields produce no harvest . . .
The Lord my God
is my strength . . .
he guides me . . .

Habacuc 3:17–19

IRRESPONSIBLE?

I shall never believe
that God
plays dice with the world.

Albert Einstein

DISSATISFIED GUEST

Father expected a good deal of God.
He didn't actually accuse God of inefficiency,
but when he prayed his tone was loud and angry,
like that of a dissatisfied guest
in a carelessly managed hotel.

Clarence Day
God and My Father

NO INTEREST

A chaplain
speaks to a condemned murderer:

"Why . . . don't you let me come
to see you?"

I explained
that I didn't believe in God.

"Are you really so sure of that?"

I said that I saw no point
in troubling my head about the matter . . .

"God can help you.
All the men I've seen in your position
turned to Him in their time of trouble."

Obviously, I replied,
they were at liberty to do so,
if they felt like it.
I, however, didn't want to be helped,
and I hadn't time to work up interest
for something that didn't interest me . . .

Albert Camus
The Stranger

WALL GRAFFITI

God doesn't
give a damn
about us.

Why should we
give a damn
about him?

UNWANTED

If God
were living on earth
people would
break his windows.

Yiddish Proverb

TWO CHOICES

Either there
isn't a God,

or if there is,
he isn't good.

SAY SOMETHING!

If there is a God
who loves man,

let him speak.
Now!

Seneca

HERE LIES GOD

Where
has
God
gone?...

I
shall
tell
you...

God
is
dead...

What
are
these
churches
now

if
they
are
not

the tombs...
of
God?

Friedrich Nietzsche

NEON GOD

And the people
bowed and prayed

To the neon God
they made . . .

Simon and Garfunkle
"Sounds of Silence"

UP-TIGHT WORLD

The main feeling you get today—
you can even see it in people's faces—
is that nearly everyone
is up-tight.
Tense vibrations are everywhere . . .

Actually, they just reflect
the sum of conflicts
and hostilities and tensions
on the individual level. . .

Maharishi Mahest Yogi of India,
founder of the worldwide
Spiritual Regeneration Movement,
believes such a tense atmosphere
and the wars
that result from it
could never happen
in a world peopled by
individuals at peace with themselves
He says,

"For the forest to be green,
the trees must be green" . . .

Paul Horn
"A Visit With India's
High-Powered New Prophet"

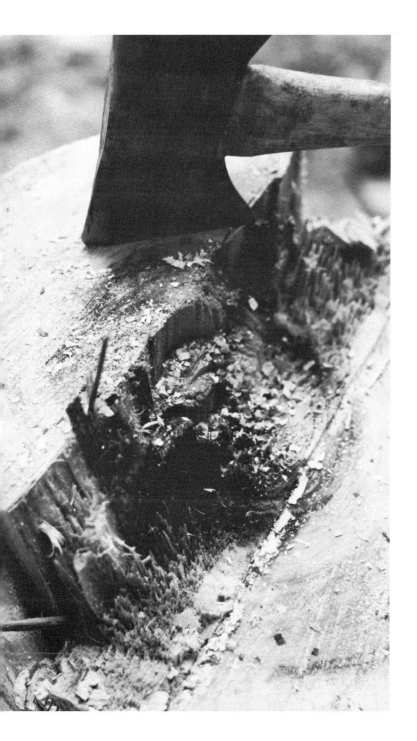

MADNESS

I have lived nearly 50 years,
and I have seen life as it is. . .

I have heard the singing from taverns
and the moans . . . on the streets.
I have been a soldier
and seen my comrades fall in battle . . .
I have held them in my arms
at the final moment.

These were men
who saw life as it is,
yet they died despairingly.
No glory, no gallant last words . . .
only their eyes filled with confusion,
whimpering the question:
"Why?"

I do not think they asked
why they were dying,
but why they had lived. . .

When life itself seems lunatic,
who knows where madness lies?
Perhaps to be too practical is madness.
To surrender dreams—
this may be madness.
To seek treasure
where there is only trash.
Too much sanity may be madness.

And maddest of all,
to see life as it is
and not as it should be.

Joe Darion
"Man of La Mancha"

13

MAN ALONE

The sanctions . . .
of being a man
are so horrendous
that it seems a madness
to relate them
to any kind of divine plan.

You are conceived
without consent,
wrenched whimpering
into an alien universe,
with your sentence
already written in the palm of
your helpless hand:
a cancer will eat your guts;
a fanatic with an axe
will cut off your head;
a tiger escaped from a village circus
will devour you;
a drunken fool with an automobile
will mow you down;
you will be burned with fire,
stifled with water;
you will decline silent
into a vegetable death;
you will live, smiling and loquacious
until a dutiful idiot
drops a hydrogen bomb
in your backyard. . .

The believers
are the lucky ones. . .
But belief is a gift . . .
If you have not the gift—
or if you lose it—
you are thrust back on reason.

Noblest of the faculties,
said the old Greeks,
but still no key
to the mystery
and the paradox
and the tragedy
of the human condition.

Morris West
''Testimony of a 20th Century Catholic''

14

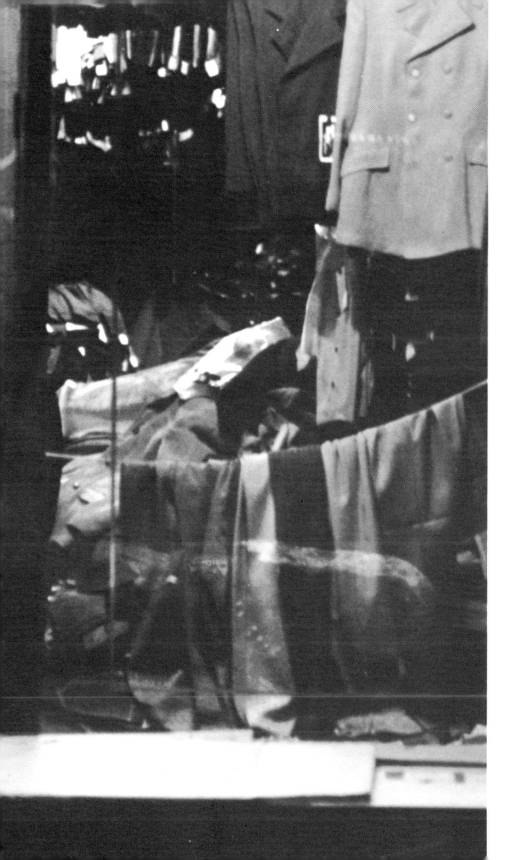

TRAGIC FIGURE

Man,
proud man!
drest in
a little brief authority. . .

Plays
such fantastic tricks
before high heaven
As make
the angels weep.

William Shakespeare
Measure for Measure

WALKING SHADOW

Tomorrow, and tomorrow,
    and tomorrow,
Creeps in this petty pace
    from day to day,
To the last syllable
    of recorded time.

And all our yesterdays
    have lighted fools
The way to dusty death.
Out, out, brief candle!

Life's but a walking shadow,
    a poor player
That struts and frets
    his hour upon the stage
And then is heard no more:
    it is a tale
Told by an idiot,
    full of sound and fury,
Signifying nothing.

William Shakespeare
Macbeth

SO MANY GIANTS

Suddenly
there are now
so many giants everywhere
so many men who think
even God looks small
when they're walking tall
and the wind of change is troubled.

Could it be
that he smiles because
he's seen this all before
and he knows the world
is finally going back to dust
and if we trust those men
who trample on the grass
emptiness is all we
can hope to ask for?

Rod McKuen
Pastorale

DIMINISHED

Omitting God
leaves man on top

but of a diminishing
universe.

Frank Sheed
Theology and Sanity

16

MAN—R.I.P.

In the nineteenth century   in the twentieth century
the problem was   the problem is
that God is dead;   that man is dead.

Erich Fromm
The Sane Society

HUMAN COGS

I grew up
as a disciple of science.
I know its fascination.
I have felt the godlike powers
man derives from his machines . . .

Now I have lived to experience
the early results of
scientific materialism.

I have watched men
turn into human cogs
in the factories they believed
would enrich their lives.
I have watched
pride in workmanship leave
and human character decline
as efficiency of production lines
increased. . .

Charles Lindbergh
Of Flight and Life

SUGAR STICKS

The soul of man
is crying for . . .
purpose or meaning:
and the scientist says

"Here is a telephone,"
or "Look, television!"—
exactly as one tries to distract
a baby crying for its mother
by offering it sugar sticks
and making funny faces at it.

The leaping stream
of invention
has served extraordinarily well
to keep man occupied,
to keep him from remembering
that which is troubling him.

Frank Sheed
Theology and Sanity

17

There is more to life
than bread and cars
and air-conditioned rooms.

Perhaps the peculiar malaise
of our day
is air-conditioned unhappiness,
the staleness and stuffiness
of machine-made routine.

Rabbi E. Borowitz

WHO?

The philosopher,
Arthur Schopenhauer,
was walking down a lonely street.
Buried in thought,
he accidentally bumped into
another pedestrian.

Angered by the jolt and
the apparent unconcern
of the philosopher,
the pedestrian shouted,
"Well, who do you think you are?"

Still lost in thought,
the philosopher said,
"Who am I?—
How I wish I knew!"

HALF-KNOWN

"Man" is our name . . .
But what is man?
He is
tremendous, puzzling and almost
nothing at the same time.
He is divided,
a stranger to himself,
riveted to his body
and nailed to his origin
and his shortcomings.
A doubtful identity.
A man is only
half-known in his own name
and soon forgotten.

Huub Osterhuis
Prayers, Poems & Songs

I don't know why
I should live
If only to die
Well, I'm not gonna buy it!
I'll never say credo
How can anybody say credo?

I want to say credo.

Leonard Bernstein
Stephen Schwartz
for *Mass*

PARADOX

Great lord of all things,
yet prey to all;
Sole judge of truth,
in endless error hurled;
The glory, jest and riddle
of the world!

Alexander Pope
An Essay on Man

LOST

Half the people
    are drowned
And the other half
    are swimming
    in the wrong direction.

Leonard Bernstein
Stephen Schwartz
for *Mass*

MAN

The truth about man is
that he has
a curious kind of dignity
but also
a curious kind of misery.

Reinhold Niebuhr

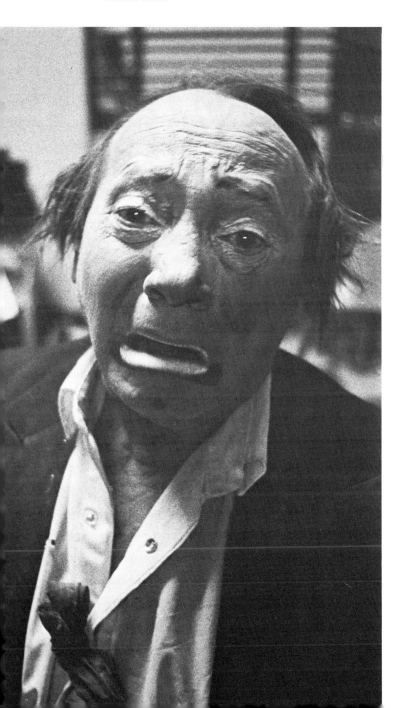

MAN IS . . .

forgiving	avenging
honest	deceptive
peaceful	violent
confident	fearful
friend	enemy
hero	coward
healer	killer
saint	sinner
happy	sad
free	enslaved
healthy	diseased
alive	dead

Why the paradox in man?

Does it
signal/suggest
something/someone
beyond/within
the clay confines of mortal man?

Lord,
make me an instrument of your peace.

Where there is hatred, let me sow love.
    Where there is injury, pardon;
    Where there is despair, hope;
    Where there is doubt, faith;
    Where there is darkness, light;
    Where there is sadness, joy. . .

For it is in giving that we receive;
it is in pardoning that we are pardoned,
and it is in dying
that we are born to eternal life.

St. Francis of Assisi

21

2

THE RIDDLE
IS THE BEGINNING

man in search

SOMETHING MISSING

. . . I emerged, at the age of 30,
a self-styled agnostic . . .

I declared that I believed in
live and let live . . .
There were no absolutes.
No more right or wrong.
And, for me, no authority and no revelation.
Certainly no supernaturalism.

Such tolerance and emancipation . . .
should have brought me happiness,
but it did not.

Fulton Oursler
"Why I Know There Is a God"

MAN IN SEARCH

What's
it
all
about? . . .

I know
there's something
much more,

Something
even non-believers
can believe in.

"Alfie"

BUICK AD

Something
to
believe
in.

BUT WHAT?

Our generation
is remarkable . . .

for the number
of people

who must believe
something

but do not know
what.

Evelyn Underhill

BELIEF

Man	As
is	he
made	believes
by	so
his	he
belief.	is.

Bhagavad-Gita

FACE TO FACE

. . . underlying all life is
the ground of doubt and self-questioning
which sooner or later
must bring us face to face
with the ultimate meaning of our life.

Thomas Merton

WHO SURVIVED?

In his book,
Man's Search For Meaning,
Viktor Frankl pointed out
that while many war prisoners
collapsed under the terror
of Nazi death camps,
not everyone did.
As a psychotherapist and a prisoner himself,
he probed for the reason.

His conclusion was
that those who survived
were men and women
who believed that their lives—
and hence, their sufferings—
had "ultimate meaning."

Dr. Frankl noted that
when a prisoner had faith,
that faith gave meaning to his existence.
It provided him with a singular energy
that helped him maintain his humanity.

GRAFFITI
(found on a concentration camp wall)

I believe in the sun
    even when it is not shining.

I believe in love
    even when I feel it not.

I believe in God
    even when he is silent.

FAITH

The life of faith is
a continually
renewed victory over doubt,

a continually
renewed grasp of meaning
in the midst of meaninglessness.

Leslie Newbign
Honest Religion for Secular Man

MAN: POINTED BEYOND HIMSELF

Viktor Frankl observed
that most prisoners passed through
three mental stages in concentration camps.

Their initial reaction was shock.
Formed in a single line, they filed by
a camp officer, who pointed to the left
for one person (crematorium)
and to the right for another (work camp).
Thousands of human lives
hinged upon the flick of his finger.

The second stage was apathy or "emotional" death.
Forced to do hard labor,
prisoners were often fed only bread
and thin soup.
They became walking skeletons.
They saw fellow prisoners cruelly beaten,
but didn't respond—even with sympathy.

Dr. Frankl observed that the sex urge
was generally absent; but religious interest
was "the most sincere imaginable."
Prisoners conducted their own services,
and the depth of their faith was surprising.

Despite deep personal suffering,
some comforted others and gave away
their own ration of bread.
In this brutal climate, some prisoners
became animals, others became saints.
Rising above suffering,
they turned life into an "inner triumph."
Dr. Frankl often cites Nietzsche's phrase:
"He who has a *why* to live for,
can bear almost any *how*."

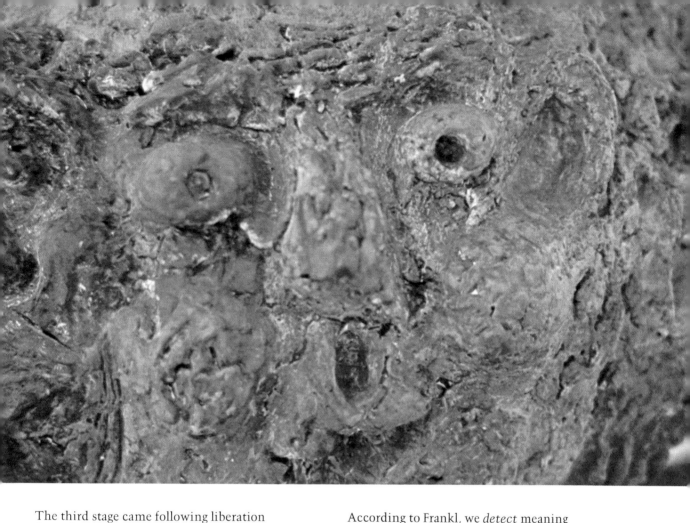

The third stage came following liberation
from the camps.
The experience was like a dream.
Some reacted bitterly, others gratefully.
Frankl's reaction was gratitude.
Shortly after his release,
he was strolling through a field of wild flowers
with birds circling overhead.
Instinctively, he knelt and prayed:
"I called to the Lord, from my narrow prison,
and he answered me in the freedom of space."
He doesn't recall how long he
knelt there, repeating those words.

Out of these prison experiences,
Dr. Frankl drew the insights for a new approach
to psychotherapy, which he calls "logotherapy."
It holds that the underlying motivation
for human behavior is the *will to meaning*—
every man's search to find a meaning to his life.

According to Frankl, we *detect* meaning
and are free to accept or to reject it.
Man is "never driven to moral behavior . . .
he decides to act morally."
Frankl holds that we can experience meaning
in one of three ways:
by performing an action (e.g., helping others),
by experiencing a value (e.g., love), or
by undergoing suffering.
What counts in suffering is *not* the suffering,
but one's attitude toward it.

Dr. Frankl denies that man is a mere product
of heredity and environment.
Man is able to surmount these.
For Frankl, the goal of human existence
is not "self-actualization," but "self transcendence"—
overcoming and surpassing one's self.

I SAID "YES"

I don't know
Who—
or what—
put the question.
I don't know
when it was put.
I don't even
remember answering.

But at some moment
I did answer *yes*
to Someone—
or Something—

and at that hour
I was certain that existence
is meaningful and that,
therefore, my life,
in self-surrender,
had a goal.

Dag Hammarskjöld,
Markings

POWER

Strong beliefs
win strong men

and then
make them stronger.

Walter Bagehot

MYSTERY

To renounce all
is to gain all;

to descend
is to rise;

to die
is to live.

Karl Rahner

INSIGHT

What seems
to be the riddle,
the abyss
of our human existence . . .
is the beginning
of eternal life.

Karl Rahner

LIKE US

Today, we try to dismiss
the "concentration camps"
as an episode of madness
in human history.

Yet, those responsible
for what happened
could all read and write.
Many lived in homes with
wall-to-wall carpeting.
Their cities were engineering masterpieces,
with modern parks and schools of music.
Their culture was the envy of Europe.

They were,
in many ways, like us.

VIET NAM

I remember this man distinctly,
holding a small child in one arm
and another child in the other,
walking toward us.

They saw us and were pleading.
The little girl was saying,
"No, no" in English.
Then all of the sudden a burst of fire
and they were cut down.

Off to the left, a group of people,
women, children and babies
were standing around . . .
I heard this fire
and here the machine gunner

had opened up on these people . . .
and they were trying to run.
I don't know how many got out . . .

There were two small children,
a very young boy and a smaller boy,
maybe 4 or 5 years old.
A guy with an M-16 fired at them,
at the first boy, and the older boy
fell over to protect the smaller boy . . .
they fired six more shots . . .
It was done very businesslike.

Peter Steinfels
"Defending Freedom,
Preventing Bloodbaths"
quoting Ronald Haeberle

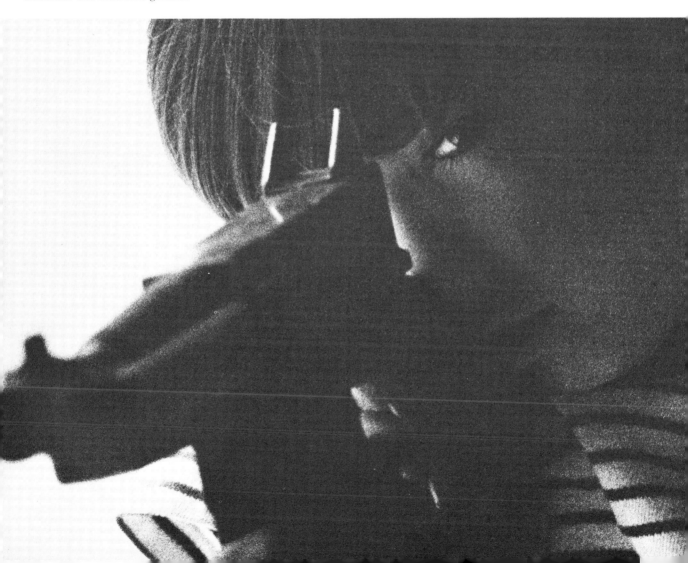

IF YOU'RE STILL THERE

As far as I know,
the most conservative estimates
of the number of Americans
who would be killed
in a major nuclear attack,
with everything working
as well as can be expected
and all foreseeable precautions taken,
run to about 50 million.

. . . next morning, if you're still there,
you read in the newspapers that
50 million people were killed.

But that isn't the way it happens . . .
Not a bang and a certain number
of corpses to bury
but a nation filled with
millions of helpless, maimed,
tortured, and doomed persons,
and the survivors huddled
with their families in shelters,
with guns
ready to fight off their neighbors
trying to get some uncontaminated
food and water.

George Wald
Nobel Prize Winner
to scientists at MIT

WARNING

More and more
of the decisions
which effect human lives
will be scientific decisions.

They must not be made
by persons who are not equipped
to understand
the moral consequences.

Dr. Aaron Ihde

NO OTHER WAY

. . . only
    with God reinstated
    in the heart of the world

    will he
    furnish mankind
    and its leaders

    the ethical guidance
    through the dangers
    and pitfalls
    of the
    Technological Revolution.

Wernher von Braun

BALANCE

Our scientific power
has outrun
our spiritual power.
We have guided missiles
and misguided men.

Science investigates;
religion interprets.
Science gives man knowledge
which is power;
religion gives man wisdom
which is control.

Martin Luther King
Strength To Love

31

BACK IN CIRCULATION

God may have been
declared dead in the 60's,
but as the 70's begin
there is considerable groundwork
being laid for his rebirth . . .

Never before in history
has a single society taken up
such a wide range of religious
and near-religious systems at once .

The searchers share
a strong motivation.
Most are keenly aware,
as Harvey Cox of Harvard puts it . . .
"while gaining the whole world,
Western man
has been losing his own soul."

Life magazine

TOUCHED BY GOD

Late have I loved You,
    O beauty ever ancient, ever new
Late have I loved You!
    And behold,
You were within, and I without,
    and without I sought You.
And deformed I ran after these forms
    of beauty You have made.

You were with me,
    and I was not with You,
those things held me back from You
    things whose only being
was to be in You.

    You called; You cried;
and You broke through my deafness
    You flashed; You shone;
and You chased away my blindness
    You became fragrant;
and I inhaled and sighed for You.
    I tasted,
and now hunger and thirst
    for You.
You touched me:
    and I burned for Your embrace

St. Augustine

MAN REVISITED

Of all the creatures
that creep and breathe on earth
there is none more wretched than man.

Homer
Iliad, c. 800 B.C.

Man has always been a wolf—
a wolf with his own refinement
who often enjoys befouling those
whom he tortures—
one could say that goodness is spread very thin
and that it manifests itself among the harshest
if only the wolf within them is asleep.
But what a light sleeper he is!

Francois Mauriac
Cain, Where Is Your Brother

We must have faith in man.
But we cannot. . .
The present world of man
has been for us a revelation of evil;
it has shattered our confidence. . .
Our vision of man has been covered over
by the unforgettable image
of the bloody ghosts in extermination camps.

Jacques Maritain
The Range of Reason

Man's radical self-assertion then blinds him
to the fact of sin,
and this is the clearest proof
that he is a fallen being.
Hence it is no good telling man that he is a sinner.

Rudolf Bultmann
Kerygma and Myth

33

SHAME/GLORY

Half dust, half duty,
unfit alike to sink or soar.

Lord Byron
Manfred

If man is not rising upwards
to be an angel,
depend on it,
he is sinking downwards
to be a devil.
He cannot stop at the beast.

Samuel Taylor Coleridge
Table Talk

Man without God
is no longer man.

Nicholas Berdyaev
The End of Our Time

What a chimera, then, is man!
what a novelty, what a monste
what a chaos,
what a subject of contradiction
what a prodigy!
A judge of all things,
feeble worm of the earth,
depository of the truth,
cloaca of uncertainty and erro:
the glory and the shame
of the universe!

Blaise Pascal
Pensees

Man is god in ruins.

Ralph Waldo Emerson
Nature

MADE FOR MORE

What is man in nature?
A nothing when compared to infinity;
a whole when compared to nothing;
a middle point between nothing and whole.

Blaise Pascal
Pensees

Man is the only animal
that laughs and weeps;
for he is the only animal
that is struck with the difference between
what things are,
and what they ought to be.

William Hazlitt
Lectures on the English Comic Writers

Under all the false,
overloaded, glittering masquerade,
there is in every man
a noble nature beneath.

B. Auerbach
On the Heights

There is a native, elemental
homing instinct in our souls
which turns us to God
as naturally as the flower turns to the sun.

Rufus M. Jones
The Inner Life

[For] if the great sun move not of himself;
but as an errand-boy in heaven;
nor one single star can revolve,
but by some invisible power;

how can this one small heart beat;
this one small brain think thoughts;
unless God does that beating,
does that thinking, does that living,
and not I.

Herman Melville
Moby Dick

Because man was made for God,
God has built man with certain powers
by which he is to take hold of God,
and certain needs
by which he is moved to exercise these powers.

Frank J. Sheed
Theology and Sanity

BUSINESS WITH GOD

The essential truth . . . is
that man is under absolute mandate
to express divinity
in his own life and his whole nature.

F. Ernest Johnson
The Social Gospel Re-examined

We and God
have business with each other;
and in opening ourselves to his influence
our deepest destiny is fulfilled.

William James
Varieties of Religious Experience

Our business on earth
is to be colonizers of heaven,
to redeem the world and set up in it
an order of life. . .

Halford E. Luccock
*Preaching Values in the
New Translation of the New Testament*

Man is the revelation
of the Infinite,
and it does not become finite in him.
It remains the Infinite.

Mark Rutherford
More Pages from a Journal

3

JOURNEY...
NOT A DESTINATION

totally other

WORDS TO PONDER

Faith will not be
restored in the West
because people
believe it to be useful.

It will return
only when
they find that it is true.

Barbara Ward
Faith and Freedom

LOST IN
CONCRETE CANYONS

Isn't the God-problem of today
totally different from
the God-problem of yesterday?

Medieval man saw God
in all the mysteries of nature:
wind, storm, and stars.

In his scientific innocence,
he tended to see God everywhere.

Today, perhaps we have
just the opposite problem.
Lost in concrete canyons
and captivated by our knowledge of science,
we tend to see God nowhere.

40

GROWTH

Our concept of God
must be extended
as the
dimensions of our world
are extended.

Teilhard de Chardin

CRUTCH CHRISTIANS

In former times,
there were many things
that men could not understand or explain.
So he used God to explain them.

Today,
as we become more educated,
we find that we need God
less and less to explain things.

Many theologians are happy about this.
Rather than fear it,
they welcome it.
They see it as a breakthrough
in helping lead people
to a better understanding of God.
Until now, perhaps our understanding of God
has tended to be somewhat simplistic.

In fact,
the popular notion of God
may be so out-of-focus in the minds
of many people,
that some theologians feel
that it would be better
to stop using the word "God" for awhile.

Theologians, like Dietrich Bonhoeffer,
lament that too many people
still treat God
merely as a "problem-solver,"
as a "bandaid" to be reached for and used
only in emergencies.
For many people
God is merely a crutch to life,
not its very source.

BAYER WORKS WONDERS

There is . . .
a peace of soul approach
to religion.

It makes of God
a gigantic Bayer aspirin . . .

Take God three times a day
and you won't feel any pain.

John Powell

LIFELESS

For some people
religion is like an artificial limb.
It has neither warmth nor life;

and although it helps them
to stumble along,
it never becomes part of them.
It must be strapped on each day.

Author unknown

THE TEST

The questions we propose are:
Does a given individual's religion
serve to break his will,
keep him at an infantile level
of development,
and enable him to avoid
the anxiety of freedom and
personal responsibility?

Or does it serve him
as a basis of meaning
which affirms his dignity and worth,
which gives him a basis for
courageous acceptance of
his limitations and normal anxiety,
but which aids him to
develop his powers,
his responsibility and his capacity
to love his fellow men?

Rollo May
Man's Search For Himself

BEYOND EXISTENCE

We often hear people say,
"Does God exist?"
We know what they mean,
but in a certain sense,
it is incorrect to speak of God as "existing."
John Ryan points this out
in his book, *The Jesus People.*

Ryan hesitates to use the word "exists"
when referring to God,
because "existing" is what creatures do.
They "stand out" (existere) from nothingness.
But God does more than that.
John Ryan suggests that we no longer
look at God as a "being."
(We should not even call him a "supreme" being.)
Rather, he is the origin and ground of all being.
For this reason, he prefers
to speak of God's "reality"
rather than of his "existence."

Touching on this same point
another theologian says:

"That is why we prefer to speak
of the 'reality of God' in which we live,
of the 'divine field' [Robinson] ...
of the 'divine milieu' [Chardin] ...
rather than of the existence of God ...

Because God does not exist as we do,
as things, people, the world exist,
and certainly not in the way we think ...
A God-object or God-person
does not exist;
we cannot imagine him as we
imagine something or someone.

On the contrary,
God is ... present
at the heart of every reality."

Robrecht Michiels
"Incarnation"

ULTIMATE CONCERN

Religion ... is shown
not in some intellectual or
verbal formulations
but in one's total orientation to life.
Religion is
whatever the individual takes to be
his ultimate concern.

One's religious attitude
is to be found
at the point where he has the conviction
that there are
values in human existence
worth living and dying for.

Rollo May
Man's Search for Himself

43

A PRESENCE

God is not an idea,
or a definition
that we have
committed to memory;

he is a presence
which we experience
in our hearts.

Louis Evely
The Gospels Without Myth

BEYOND THOUGHT

God is
inexpressible.
It is easier for us
to say
what he is not than
what he is. . .

Nothing
is comparable
to him . . .

If you could
conceive of him
you would
conceive of something
other than God.

He is not at all
what you have
conceived him to be.

St. Augustine

BIG DIFFERENCE

What we mean
when we say that God is personal
is that he is more like a person
than he is like anything else
in our experience.

Kirby Page

ATTIC ATHEIST

The atheist
staring from his attic window
is often nearer to God

than the believer
caught up in his own
false image of God.

Martin Buber

TURNABOUT

The Book of Genesis says
that God created man
to his image and likeness.

It seems that
the most perduring heresy
in all of Christian history
has been this—

that man has reversed Genesis—
man has made God
to his image and likeness.

John Powell

EASIER

Man finds it difficult to believe
that this utter mystery
is close to us
and not remote,
is love
and not a spurning judgment.

Karl Rahner

GRAFFITI
(at a women's lib convention)

I went to heaven
and saw God.

Wow, would you believe:
She's black.

WOULD YOU BELIEVE . . .

God does not believe
in our God.

Jules Renard

INCREDIBLE

Like some kind of heavenly dictator,
God was thought of
as permitting evil in the present,
for the sake of a greater good
to be achieved in the future.

Even Auschwitz,
according to this theology,
had a place in divine providence.
Today many find this view
of divine providence incredible.

Gregory Baum
Man Becoming

CARICATURE

Man distinguishes reality
through his senses;
he expresses reality
through images.

Through the centuries
man has created images of God.
Some are artists like Michelangelo,
the craftsmen of Chartres,
El Greco.

Though all these images are diverse,
strict reliance on them is chancy.
To your mind, do these images tend
to clarify or caricature God?

It is the nature of the image
to concretize, to isolate, to intensify.
Artists, theologians, poets
have expressed themselves through images
because images are intense and vivid.
But they are also specific,
perhaps too limiting.

The traditional images attribute
human qualities to God.
He demands, he permits, he punishes.
But how accurate
are these images and attributes
when used of God?
Could it be that, today, they tend to distort
rather than clarify the reality of God?

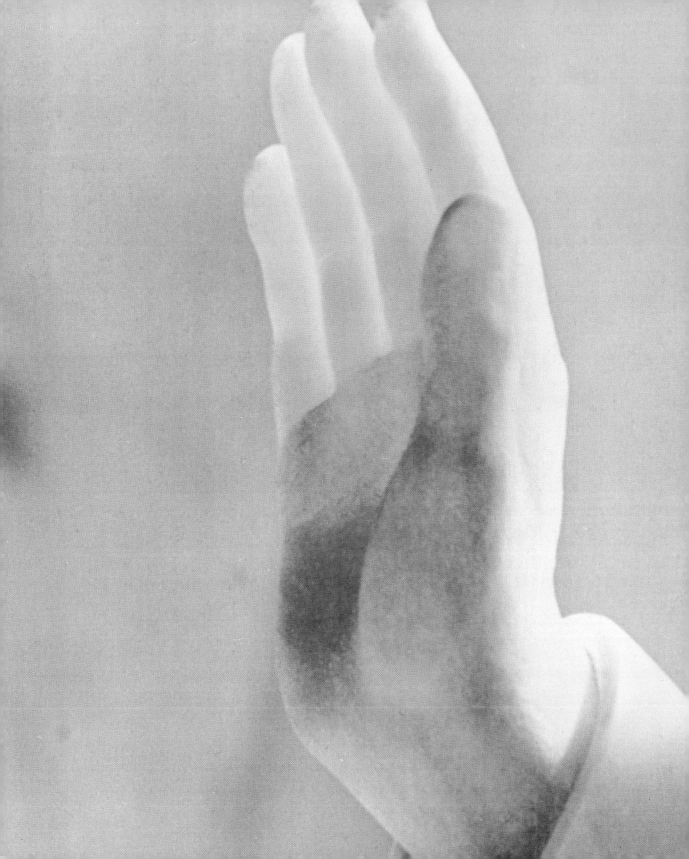

GOD GRAMMAR

Suspend for a moment
all traditional images of God.
How do you image-ine him?

Some see God as *being*—
which involves process, motion.
For them the traditional images
are inadequate for they are static.

Being is a difficult state
to capture in a single image.
For some moving images are necessary
to convey God—
kinetic sculpture, film,
multiple images and colors.

"For God, to me, it seems,
is a verb,
not a noun."

Buckminster Fuller

SHATTERING

A religion invented
by intellectuals for intellectuals . . .
will almost certainly
have the smell of paper flowers.

A way of life
arises out of shattering experiences—
experiences which
shatter an accepted sense of reality
and cry out for a new one.

There has been no lack of
such experiences in our century.
What we lack is
the knack of interpretation:
the genius, perhaps, to *allow* ourselves
to be genuinely shattered
and to find the new form
which expresses our new identity.

Michael Novak

NO ROOM—ANYWHERE

Until the last recesses
of the cosmos had been explored
or where capable of being explored . . .
it was possible to locate God mentally
in some . . . [unknown place].

But now it seems there is no room for him,
not merely in the inn,
but in the entire universe:
for there are no vacant places left.

John Robinson
Honest to God

If it is impossible to try
to fit God into the
human thought category
of "person,"
it is also inaccurate
to think of God as
hovering somewhere
above the world.

Theologians today think
God lives in our midst:
the foundation and root
of all that is,
the one from whom the
world has its origin
and towards whom the world
is tending in fulfillment.

In this thinking, God would be
the heart and center of all reality.

The Biblical basis for this
is found in the Psalms.
There the inspired poet says:
"God knows my name;
he holds the world in his hands."

For the psalmist,
God is not a super-person
or a super-idea.
He is a concrete presence
flooding all reality and life.

49

IT TOOK TIME

In biblical times
almost every nation
worshipped a variety of gods.

There were sun gods, rain gods,
fertility gods.

At first Israel thought and spoke
of their God—Yahweh—
in much the same way
as other peoples spoke of their gods
Yahweh was an "angry" God,
a "wrathful" God,
a God of human emotions.

As time passed
Israel developed the concept
of Yahweh as totally different
from all other gods.
They still used conventional
human language to describe him,
but their idea of him clarified.

They arrived at a
monotheistic belief:
for the Israelite
Yahweh was not only
greater than any other,
but, in fact, the only God.

DEATH/BIRTH

The experience
of the death of the gods,
or of God,
is the consequence
of an abrupt transition
which causes
the traditional symbols
to collapse
since they no longer
illuminate
the shifting social reality.

Harvey Cox

Men
with new consciousnesses
are new men

and new men
need to declare
the old gods dead. . .

A death-of-god era
is also
a god-building era.

Harvey Wheeler
Center magazine

GOD-TALK

What unites the
various contemporary approaches
to the God problem is . . .
that the primary question
has become

not what God is, but how
men are justified in using the word

Time magazine

FOUR OPTIONS

Today some theologians see
four options open
in handling the God-problem.
Time magazine listed them this way:

- stop talking about God for a while,
- stick to what the Bible says,
- formulate a new image and concept
  of God using contemporary thought
  categories, or
- simply point the way to
  areas of human experience
  that indicate the presence
  of something beyond man in life.

AGREEMENT

Edward Echlin cites these areas
of emerging agreement
concerning God-talk and God-thought:

• Any concept or symbol of God is . . .
inadequate to capture God.

• God remains
transcendent [he surpasses human life]
and immanent [he is intimately
involved in human life],
but today's God-talk,
while affirming transcendence
stresses God's immanence.

• God is seen
not at detached or unconcerned,
but as involved with men.

• While conceding that
the idea of a "person" does not
adequately grasp God and that
the very idea of person is still mysterious,
theologians refer to God
as profoundly personal. . .

• God is ultimate,
the unconditioned, the ground, source,
and goal of all things.
God is the giver of ultimate meaning;
he is what Tillich saw as ultimate concern.
God is real in the most ultimate sense.
He is *ultimate* reality.

• God has a future.
The idea of God will develop and clarify
as God discloses himself
more and more in the future.
By responding to God men are active agents
in bringing to pass the future of God.

"Finding God in the City"

BELIEVING IN
THE INDEFINABLE

Dr. Warren Weaver,
a mathematician, writes:

I think a scientist
has a real advantage
in any struggle to conceive
and believe in God.
For he is expert in
seeing the unseeable and in
believing the essentially indefinable. . .

Now, no scientist has ever seen
an electron.
"Electron" is simply the name
for a consistent set of things
that happen in certain circumstances.
For a while, physicists thought
that the electron was a particle.
Then they realized
that electrons are wave motions.
Today they think of electrons
as being both (or either)
particles and waves.
Yet nothing seems to them more "real."

All this may seem ridiculous to you.
But just as there are
various complex ideas about the electron—
it is sometimes one thing,
sometimes another;
it can't be seen,
and can't be precisely located—
so there are
various ideas about God.
He, too, I think, can neither be
seen nor precisely located.

NO CROSSWORD PUZZLE

There is something
marvelously inviting to the mind
about someone
"of whom we can know something,
but whom we cannot wholly know,
in the knowledge of whom we can grow,
yet the truth of whose being
we can never exhaust;

we shall never
have to throw God away
like a solved crossword puzzle."

Frank Sheed
Theology and Sanity

THE REAL LEAPS

Dr. Charles Townes,
Nobel Prize winner for his work on
the laser and maser, writes:

To me, science and religion
are . . . very similar. . .
If we compare
how great scientific ideas arrive,
they look remarkably like
religious revelation
viewed in a non-mystical way. . .

The great scientific discoveries,
the real leaps,
do not usually come from
so-called scientific method but
by revelations which are just as real.

Think magazine

Dr. Townes' insight into the laser
came while he was sitting
on a park bench looking at flowers.

Dr. Wernher von Braun,
the leading U.S. space expert, says:
While science is not religion,
it is a religious activity by
its presuppositions,
its methods of working and
its search for truth.

The priest-scientist, Teilhard de Chardin, notes:
Perhaps we shall end by perceiving
that the great object
unconsciously pursued by science
is nothing else than the discovery of God.

Charles Coulson says poetically:
Science is helping us put a face on God.

THE INDEFINABLE

We know God easily
if we do not
constrain ourselves
to define him

Joseph Joubert

God has suffered
from too many attempts
to define the indefinable.

Jerry Handspicker

JOURNEY—
NOT A DESTINATION

God,
I don't know
if I know you or not.
They say you are
as close to me
as I am to myself.
But you might as well be
a stranger in the mist.
If wishes were real
you would be more real to me
than flesh and blood.

Could it be that here
is where I lose the trail:
I look for you
the way I picture you,
rather than
the way you really are?

Do I look up when, perhaps,
you have no direction?
Should I even look—
can the eye see the eye?
Am I looking for
color in a song;
or sound in a sunset;
or trying to cup-in-hand
sweetness and sorrow?

Am I searching for something
when perhaps that "something"
is the search?
Could it be
that while I walk in flesh,
you will never be a destination—
only a journey?

What if I found you?
That would be heaven!
But can heaven be on earth?
Can east be in the west?

When does the quest
cease to be the question
and become the answer?

Or, perhaps, that is it:
the question is the answer;
the search is the discovery.
In going, I am already there–
as "there" as any traveler
can expect to be.

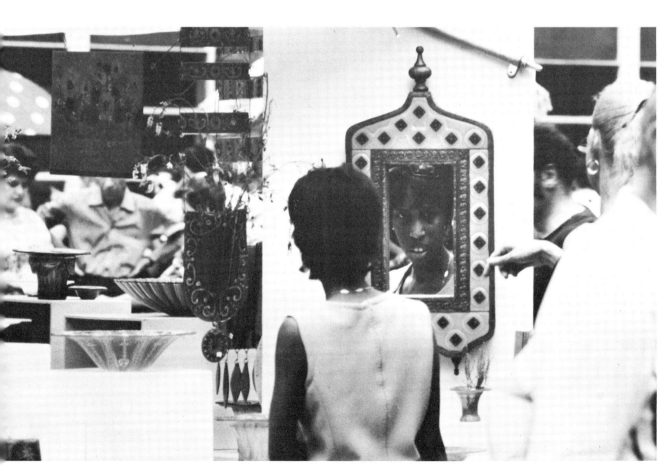

CEASELESS JOURNEY

The earthly goal
of the journey toward God
is not to find him
in some blinding,
beatific experience,
but to struggle ceaselessly
to continue the journey.

John Shea
The Critic

ONLY THEN

There comes a time
in every life
to forget words,
to set aside names,
to turn the mirror face to the wall,
to be blind with one's earthly eyes
and to dedicate oneself to silence
with all its dangers.

Only then can one recognize
what trifling . . . empty words
are often used of God.

Ladislaus Boros
God Is With Us

PURSUIT OF GOD

There are
innumerable definitions of God
because his manifestations
are innumerable.
They overwhelm me . . . stun me.

Mohandus K. Gandhi
My Experiment with Truth

I have not found him.
I am prepared to sacrifice
the things dearest to me
in pursuit of this quest.

Mohandus K. Gandhi
My Experiment with Truth

Whoever seeks the Truth
or loves the Good
or strives in prose or in verse,
in bronze, in marble, on canvas,
or through the insubstantial, ethereal,
elusive, evanescent medium of melody and harmony,
to express the Beautiful,
is really,
though he know it not,
striving for God.

James M. Gillis
If Not Christianity, What?

4

AT HALF PAST TWELVE
AT NIGHT

experience of the other

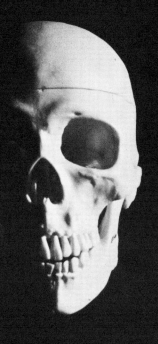

SILENT GOD

In the screenplay, *The Seventh Seal*,
a Knight talks with Death.
The discussion concerns God.

Knight: Why should he hide himself
in a mist . . .
I want knowledge . . .
I want God to stretch out his hand
toward me, reveal himself, and
speak to me.

Death: But He remains silent.

Knight: I call out to Him in the dark
but no one seems to be there.

Death: Perhaps no one is there.

Four Screenplays of Ingmar Bergman

DID HE?

The short story, "Pigeon Feathers,"
centers around a young boy, David.
In the story, David experiences
doubt about the faith he grew up with.

He wrestles desperately with the problem,
but with no success.
Then, one night in bed,
he decides upon an experiment,
as a kind of last resort.

"Though the experiment frightened him,
he lifted his hands
high into the darkness above his face
and begged Christ to touch them.
Not hard or long: the faintest, quickest gr
would be final for a lifetime.

His hands waited in the air,
itself a substance,
which seemed to move through his finger
or was it the pressure of his pulse.

He returned his hands beneath the covers
uncertain
if they had been touched or not."

John Updike
Pigeon Feathers and Other Stories

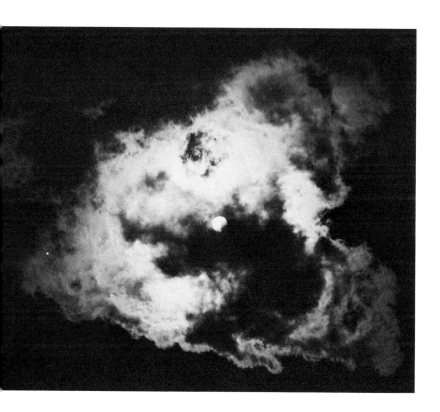

DID I?

I had suddenly an odd . . .
desire . . . and so
stepping into the moonlit road,
I knelt in the dust . . .

There was
no God in the sky,
no God in myself,
no conviction in myself that
I had the power
to believe in God,
and so I merely knelt
in the dust in silence
and no words
came to my lips.

Did I worship
merely the dust
under my knees?

Sherwood Anderson
A Story Teller's Tale

TO NO AVAIL

I tried to reason myself back to
a first cause and first motion,
as a foundling might reason himself
back to the existence of a father.
He must have existed,
all children have fathers.

But who was he?
What was his name?
What did he look like?
Did he love me—
or had he forgotten me forever?

Morris West
The Devil's Advocate

IMPOSSIBLE

. . . any appeal to a special revelation
is impossible and even senseless

unless a man
'through his own human capacities
and without any special revelation' . . .

can satisfy himself
of the existence of a personal God
from his own experience.

Edward Schillebeeckx
God and Man

61

WHERE ARE YOU GOD?

Isn't there a bit of the Knight,
David, and
"the man kneeling in the dust"
in all of us?

Don't we want God
to reach out and "touch" us,
but he doesn't?
Don't we thirst for some "sign,"
some vivid "experience of God,"
and it never comes?

SIGNALS OF TRANSCENDENCE

Do we look for God
too much in the "strange,"
and not enough in the "common?"
In his book, *A Rumor Of Angels*,
Peter Berger talks about
"signals of transcendence."

A signal of transcendence
is a phenomenon in life,
pointing "beyond" itself.
Berger cites these examples of
hope and humor:

Hope is the spirit of man
saying "no" to death.
The reality of hope seems to "signal"
that there is something beyond life.

The fact that man hopes
indicates that he intuits
a "something" to be hoped for.
Without this "something,"
human hope is without any ultimate justification.

Humor reflects
the imprisonment of the human spirit
in the world.
At the same time,
it implies that this imprisonment is not final.
It will eventually win freedom.
As Stephen Tonsor has observed,
"The comic implies that
tragedy will be overcome,
that redemption is nearer
than we first thought."

EXPERIENCING GOD

I sometimes get the impression
that people are thirsting for direct . . .
almost visual encounter with God . . .

I stand ready to be corrected on this,
but I would submit that in this life
it is only in and through his *effects*
that God is present to us.

James Connor
"The Experience of God"

TRANSFORMED

Some may call experiences
of *God's effects* the experience of God,
but that in my opinion
is stretching the meaning of the word . . .

Faith is not an experience of God;
but given faith, experience is transformed
into God's self-manifestation.

Christopher Kiesling
Chicago Studies

HIS SIGN

[God] exists within us
even more intimately
than we exist within ourselve

His kingdom is within us;
and when he wishes
to show himself,
he chooses a beggar,
a child, a sinner;
and fills that beggar,
that child, that sinner
with love.

Love is his sign.
And by that sign
we shall all know him.

Louis Evely
The Gospels Without Myth

MYSTERIOUS PRESENCE

To meet
a human being

is an opportunity
to sense

the image of God,
the presence of God.

Abraham Heschel

NO SUCH THING

People who tell me
there is no God
are like
a six-year-old boy saying
there is no such thing
as passionate love—
they just haven't
experienced it.

William Alfred

HEART

It is the heart
that experiences God,
not the reason.

Blaise Pascal

LOVE IS

Love is the only force
that can make things one
without destroying them.

Teilhard de Chardin

God is love,
and whoever lives in love
lives in God
and God lives in him.

I John 4:16

CALL TO TRANSCENDENCE

There are times when I experience
an intense . . . incapacity . . .
This feeling . . . occurs most sharply . . .
when others are looking to me . . .
to be someone that they
have every right to expect, but which
I know in my heart I am not . . .

In these moods . . .
what emerges in me
is a deep . . . hunger . . .
to open my cold, discouraged . . . heart
to God within me who I believe can
and will enliven me . . . purge me . . .

I believe with utter confidence
that this hunger and desire
is wrought in me by God . . .
calling me . . . to be myself
in and with him . . .

Another way in which I believe
I experience God in my life is
in and through . . . unsettlement . . .
It is a stimulus which shakes complacency . . .
It acknowledges that life is good,
but warns that it must be better . . .
It calls me to all sorts of things
which I would rather not do . . .

In each of these experiences there is
a clear impression not only of *being moved* . . .
but also of being *moved* . . .
beyond self-interest or selfishness
towards self-transcendence.

James Connor
"The Experience of God"

Speaking to
the Little Prince
about love and life,
the Fox says:
"And now here
is my secret,
a very simple secret:
It is only
with the heart
that one can see rightly;
What is essential
is invisible
to the eye."

Antoine de Saint-Exupery
The Little Prince

NOBODY WORKED IT

There are a variety of times . . .
in which I believe
I have experienced God . . .
certain liturgies,
certain small group discussions . . .
certain conversations . . .
what moves me in each instance
is the realization of the sheer goodness
of the people involved . . .
Call it, if you will,
an experience of communion.
It happens; nobody worked at it.

James Connor
"The Experience of God"

A BEYOND "WITHIN"

What is this mysterious presence
within us
that we call "conscience?"

It seems to direct us beyond ourselves
to a greater horizon.
Does it really matter
that sometimes we disagree
about what conscience seems to say
about *this* or *that* particular act?

Don't most of us
experience some kind of call
to an ultimate order
that exists beyond our own designs?

CONSCIENCE

It praises, it blames,
it promises, it threatens,
it implies a future and
it witnesses to the unseen.

It is more than man's own self.
The man himself
has no power over it, or
only with extreme difficulty;
he may not make it,
he cannot destroy it,
he may refuse to use it,
but it remains . . .
its very existence throws us
out of ourselves, to go seek him
in the heights and depths,
whose Voice it is.

John Henry Newman
Apologia Pro Vita Sua

WITHIN GRASP

When we ask,
"Why am I?"
"What should I become and be?"
"What is the meaning
of my life?"—

then we are exploring . . .
the region of our experience
where God *may* be known . . .

Langdon Gilkey

UPON THEIR HEARTS

Behold the days are coming,
says the Lord,
when I will . . . put my law within them,
and will write it upon their hearts;
and I will be their God,
and they shall be my people.

And no longer shall each man teach
his neighbor and each his brother saying,
''know the Lord,''
for they shall all know me,
from the least of them to the greatest.

Jeremiah 31:31,33–34

Moses said:

This command which I enjoin on you today
is not too mysterious and remote for you.
It is not up in the sky, that you should say,
'Who will go up in the sky and get it for us
and tell us of it, that we may carry it out?'
Nor is it across the sea, that you should say,
'Who will cross the sea to get it for us
and tell us of it, that we may carry it out?'

No, it is something very near to you, already
in your mouths, and in your hearts;
you have only to carry it out.

Deuteronomy 30:10–14

WHY?

I am deeply moved by the tragic . . .
I feel it in the icy chill
of distance and suspicion
which sometimes walls me off
from a fellow human being . . .
I feel pained . . . and guilty . . .
Why can't we live—and love—
as brothers? . . .

In the face of an aspiration
for peace and community,
I feel the tragedy of hostility . . .

This positive call, aspiration, and urging,
in whose light I see and suffer its absence,
I believe to be the effect
of God's active presence within me.

James Connor
''The Experience of God''

MAN IN SEARCH

Man must evolve for all human conflict
a method that rejects
revenge, agression and retaliation.
The foundation of such a method
is love.

Martin Luther King

CRISIS TIMES

In times of
crisis and tragedy,
aren't there moments when you feel
utterly abandoned
or completely helpless?
Aren't there times when you feel crushed
by events or by people?
It is then that we anxiously
seek to know the meaning of
existence.

Crisis times set at zero
the ordinary concerns of daily life.
They invite us to ponder
with proper awe and seriousness
the real mystery of life.

ZERO MOMENTS

William James,
father of American psychology,
felt that the most convincing evidence of God
"lies primarily in inner personal experience,"
and the starting point is
the sense of emptiness and frustration.
James researched his thesis and published his
findings in *Varieties of Religious Experience*
and *Pragmatism*.

"As a young man, he [James] had experienced . . .
poor health . . . and this caused him
frequent periods of depression
and discouragement.
About the same time, he seems to have
gone through a spiritual crisis,
which manifested itself
in a lack of motivation and purpose.
Slowly he began to realize that
he needed a unifying philosophy of life.

All this brought to a focus
the sense of incompleteness that
James found in the depths of his being
as he looked at the world around him . . .
Sorrow, disappointment, failure,
physical pain,
all led James to the conclusion that
'natural goods perish;
riches take wings; fame is a breath;
love is a cheat; youth and health and pleasure
vanish.' . . .

Bill W., a co-founder of Alcoholics Anonymous,
was still trying to fight his way back to sobriety,
when he happened upon a copy
of James' *Varieties of Religious Experience*.

Perhaps more than most others,
Bill W. felt the frustration and anguish
consequent upon human weakness and misery.
He took seriously
James' observation that truly transforming
spiritual experiences
are nearly always founded on calamity and
collapse.
Following through on this lesson learned
from *Varieties of Religious Experience*,
Bill W. writes:

'Complete hopelessness and
deflation at depth were almost always required
to make the recipient of the religious
experience ready.
The significance of all this burst upon me.
Deflation at depth—
yes, that was *it*.
Exactly that had happened to me.'

For Bill W. and others like him,
alcoholism was the starting point
on the way to God and to sobriety.
Their affliction was not so much
the cause of their return to God as its occasion."

Robert Roth
"William James and Alcoholics Anonymous"

START HERE

The first step
in filling a container

is to be sure
it is empty.

Author unknown

69

SOMETHING "MORE"

At the end of his book,
The Varieties of Religious Experience,
William James draws these conclusions:

• "That the visible world
is part of a more spiritual universe
from which it draws its chief significance."

   In each case studied,
   James found that over and above
   the explainable biological and
   psychological facts of each experience
   was a greater dimension, a "more,"
   which produced the values and aspirations
   which flowed out of each religious experience.

• "That union or harmonious relation
with that higher universe is our true end."

   James concludes:
   "We and God have business with each other;
   and in opening ourselves to his influence
   our deepest destiny is fulfilled."

   These values and aspirations have a real impact
   on the development and direction
   of our personalities.
   For we are "turned into new men."

• "That prayer or inner communion
with the spirit of this 'higher universe' . . .
is a process wherein . . .
spiritual energy flows in and produces effects,
psychological or material,
within the phenomenal world."

LIFE/DEATH—
WITHOUT PURPOSE

At 15 I joined the Communist party.
I soon had interest in nothing else.
I read Marx, Engels, Lenin.
All my teachers were professed atheists.
For me there was no "problem" of religion.
I was against it.

In my regular schooling I learned
the traditional metaphysical proofs for
the existence of God.
But my knowledge did not concern *me* . . .

I felt no need of God because the life I had
seemed enough.

The psychological content of my atheism changed
when I broke with the Communist party.
The official heirs of the October revolution
were straying from the ideal which had attracted me.
I was still convinced that communism alone
could realize
the ideal of universal fraternity and justice.
I accused the Stalinists of treason . . .

Death for the cause,
on the barricades or before a firing squad,
had seemed worthwhile,
but life without purpose,
like death without purpose, seemed meaningless . . .

More and more frequently I questioned myself
about the meaning of this life.
It did not seem logical that beings endowed
with a capacity for thinking and loving
could be thrown into an absurd universe,
where there was nothing to think,
nothing to love,
nothing to hope for.
It was with these psychological dispositions
that I encountered the Christian message
and accepted it . . .

Ignace Lepp
Atheism in Our Time

LIKE A SHADOW

As for man,
his life is like grass;
he grows and flourishes
like a wild flower.
Then the wind blows on it,
and it is gone,
and no one sees it again.

Psalm 103:15–17

Indeed every living man
is no more
than a puff of wind,
no more than
a shadow! . . .

What, then,
can I hope for, Lord?
I put my hope in you.

Psalm 39:5–7

BUT NOW I AM AFRAID

One night toward the end of January
I settled into bed late, after a strenuous day.
Coretta had already fallen asleep
and just as I was about to doze off
the telephone rang.

An angry voice said,
"Listen, nigger, we've taken all we want from you;
before next week you'll be sorry
you ever came to Montgomery."
I hung up, but I couldn't sleep.
It seemed that all of my fears had
come down on me at once.
I had reached the saturation point.

I got out of bed and began to walk the floor.
Finally I went to the kitchen
and heated a pot of coffee.
I was ready to give up.
With my cup of coffee sitting untouched before me
I tried to think of a way to move out of the picture
without appearing a coward.

In this state of exhaustion,
when my courage had all but gone,
I decided to take my problem to God.
With my head in my hands, I bowed
over the kitchen table and prayed aloud.
The words I spoke to God that midnight
are still vivid in my memory.

"I am here taking a stand
for what I believe is right.
But now I am afraid.
The people are looking to me for leadership,
and if I stand before them
without strength and courage,
they too will falter.
I am at the end of my powers.
I have nothing left. I've come to the point
where I can't face it alone."
At that moment I experienced the
presence of the Divine as I had never
experienced Him before.

Martin Luther King
Stride Toward Freedom

ALL MY TRUST

I knew that defeat in a great battle
in Northern soil involved loss of Washington . . .
I went to my room
and got down on my knees in prayer.

Never before
had I prayed with as much earnestness.
I wish I could repeat my prayer.
I felt that I must put all my trust
in Almighty God . . .

I had no misgivings about the result.

Abraham Lincoln

THEY CALLED
TO THE LORD

Some wandered
in the trackless desert
and could not find their way . . .

Some were living
in gloom and darkness,
prisoners suffering in chains . . .

Some were sick
because of their sins,
suffering
because of their evil . . .

In their trouble
they called to the Lord,
and he saved them
from their distress.

Psalm 107:4–28

FIRE AT NIGHT

Blaise Pascal,
the philosopher-mathematician,
had an experience
that changed the course of his life.
Pascal wrote out the experience
and sewed it into his clothes.
It was found on his body
when he died nine years later.
It reads:

The year of the Lord 1654.
Monday, 23 November,
from about half past ten
in the evening until about
half past twelve at night: fire.

God of Abraham,
God of Isaac,
God of Jacob,
not the God
of philosophers and scholars.

Certainty, joy, peace.
God of Jesus Christ.
He is only found along the ways
that are taught in the gospel.

Tears of joy.
I had parted from him.
Let me never be separated
from him.
Surrender to Jesus Christ.

quoted by Huub Oosterhuis
Prayers, Poems & Songs

5

CUT THE STRING

belief in the other

A TIME . . .

There is a time to live
and a time to die;
A time for doing,
for experiencing,
for assimilating,

A time to despair,
To doubt,
To be confident:

A time for childhood,
for youth,
for manhood,
for age:

A time to remember God,
To miss God,
To wait for God.

John S. Dunne
A Search for God in Time and Memory
Ecclesiastes 3:1ff

A KIND OF DEATH

. . . "I don't know what's gone wrong,
but I just don't believe like I used to.
When I was in grade school
and for the first couple of years
of high school I was real religious,
and now I just don't seem to care."

The young person feels sick at heart;
he feels deeply guilty.
Yet the chances are that the only thing
wrong with him is that he's growing up.
He suffers from being a
human being subject to change.

This isn't to gloss over the pain
that is almost inevitable.

Nor is it to water down the dangers of
the experience or its riskiness.
It's simply to state a fact of our humanity
that will challenge some and petrify others.

The youth is passing from one stage
of his life to another.
There is a kind of death involved in the transition,
for one level must die
if the other is to be born healthy.
Usually there is no clear moment of death.
There is a kind of overlap, one stage of life
slowly losing its grip
while another begins a slow rise to dominance.

John J. Kirvan
"The Restless Believers"

DARK PASSAGE

The corridor leading
from childhood faith
to adult faith
can be narrow and dark.

The passage
from being Religious
by culture
to becoming Religious
by conviction
can be disturbing and agonizing.

MY DANCING DOUBT

. . . I wore the mask that nature handed out
of being English, old or young, a male,
married or otherwise.

Where was I really living all the while?
I played the conscientious hypocrite
and persecuted doubt

Which flowered like a faith turned inside out,
dancing and lyrical, and made a mock
of all my history . . .

Sydney Carter
Nothing Fixed or Final

I GUESS
I THINK TOO MUCH . . .

"I hate to say this,
but sometimes I get to wondering
if there is a God—and it scares me! . . .
Maybe I think too much—
I don't know," he said.

"How do you mean?" I asked.

"Oh, if I would just quit thinking about
these things—you know,
how God can hear everybody's
prayers at the same time
and how a dead person can live again—
things like that."

"Have you tried to quit thinking
about these things?"

"Yes, I guess I have," he said.

William Hulme
I Hate to Bother You, But . . .

NOT REJECTION

When a person begins
to question the faith it is
"only too easy to teach him
to repress these doubts
and to rationalize his difficulties.
This is a mistake.
It should be pointed out to him
that doubt in his mind
is really a question:
a seeking of further enlightenment,
not a rejection of the faith."

E. F. Doherty

TURNING POINT

It is precisely when faith
"is exempted from the normal
human questioning process
it passes into superstition.
It is precisely when a person
stops asking
what the point of prayer is,
that he begins to regard it as magical . . ."

Vincent Rugiero

NEW FAITH DEPTH

When we question honestly,
we probe more deeply into reality.
Questioning clarifies.
Clarification, in turn,
deepens faith understanding.

Consider prayer.
When we were children,
many of us probably prayed to God
routinely and without much thought
of what we were doing.
Then, perhaps, doubts arose to force us
to rethink the whole idea of prayer.

As a result of our thinking,
we, perhaps, gained a deeper insight
into the mystery and nature of prayer.

Before we questioned prayer,
it may have been merely a habit-response.
Now it becomes a personal choice.
It becomes more human, more conscious,
more reflective.

NEW FAITH SCOPE

Questioning can also widen faith understanding.
Years ago, many believers questioned
whether evolution and religion were compatible.
When they explored the problem
more deeply, however, they discovered
that evolution was not only consistent
with religion, but also more in keeping with it.

A deeper study of Scripture
shows that creation is an on-going process,
not a finished or static event.
Because of questioning,
faith was clarified and expanded
to embrace greater horizons and ideas.

SIGN OF LIFE

There lives
more faith
in honest doubt . . .
than in half the creeds.

Alfred Tennyson

BREAKTHROUGH

Most young people
expect adult church-goers
to be honest, responsible persons.

What happens, then, when a young person
discovers that not a few church-goers may be
contaminated with prejudice
and involved in hypocrisy?

Understandably, he may conclude
that adults,
even church-goers,
cannot be trusted completely.

Such an awareness can lead to a crisis,
not only regarding faith in people,
but also faith in God and religion.

THEY MISS THE POINT

Those who think that
a young person
is losing his faith,
merely because he questions it,
are missing the point.
To question is to care.

At some point in life,
don't we inevitably meet some sort of
stumbling block
that threatens to shatter everything
we once accepted?

But, just as often,
is not this stumbling block
a stepping stone in disguise?

Consider this phenomenon.
When a bone is broken,
it is painful.
But with the process of time
it grows back stronger
at the point of break
than it was in the beginning.

Can this not be applied
to faith as well?

TAKE YOUR CHOICE

Doubt comes in
at the window

when inquiry is denied
at the door.

Benjamin Jowert

R.I.P.

When faith
becomes blind,
it dies.

Mohandas Gandhi

MISTAKEN IDENTITY

Without a
consciousness of truth itself
doubt of truth
would be impossible.

Paul Tillich

Doubt is a pain
too lonely to know
that faith
is his twin brother.

Kahlil Gibran

LIFE IS RISK

How can we be sure of anything
    the tide changes.
The wind that made the grain wave gently yesterday
    blows down the trees tomorrow.
And the sea sends sailors crashing on the rocks,
    as easily as it guides them safely home.

    I love the sea
But it doesn't make me less afraid of it.
    I love you
But I'm not always sure of what you are
    And how you feel.

Rod McKuen

NITTY-GRITTY

Being human
means being limited.
This is part of the "nitty-gritty"
of the human condition.

Accepting our human condition
means that our understanding of
the deepest realities of life
will always be inadequate or in shadow.

NO EXIT

If there is a lesson
in the history of religious experience
in modern times,
it is that the quest for certainty
is self-defeating.

The more earnestly a man
seeks for certainty,
the more uncertain he becomes:
the more strenuously
he tries to remove all doubt,
the more doubt he experiences.

John S. Dunne
A Search for God in Time and Memory

KIERKEGAARD'S PARABLE

Once there was a king
who loved a humble maiden.
This king was so powerful and well established
that he could not marry her
without being forced to abdicate.
If he were to marry her,
the king knew that he would make her forever grateful.

It occurred to him, though,
that something would be wanting in her happiness.
She would always admire him and thank him,
but she would not be able to love him,
for the inequality between them would be too great,
and she would never be able to forget
her humble origin and her debt of gratitude.

So he decided upon another way.
Instead of making her queen,
he would renounce the kingship.
He would become a commoner
and then offer her his love.
In doing this he realized that he was taking a great risk.
He was doing something that would be foolish
in the eyes of most people in his kingdom,
perhaps even in her eyes.
He would lose the kingship,
and he might also be rejected by her,
especially if she were disappointed at not becoming queen.

Yet he decided to take this risk.
It was better, he believed, to risk everything
in order to make love possible.

John S. Dunne
A Search For God In Time And Memory

THE FAITH CAME FIRST

The faith came first.
In the beginning was
the way that I believe
and after that
came all that I believe in. . .

By faith I test
the gospel of St. Matthew,
Michelangelo,
Bach or the Beatles
but the faith came first, I see
no other rock
but this to
build upon.

Sydney Carter
Nothing Fixed or Final

CHOOSE ONE

There are essentially
four kinds of risk:

The risk one must accept.
The risk one can afford to take.
The risk one cannot afford to take.
The risk one cannot afford not to take.

Peter Drucker

THE STRING

There's one thing
missing in you, Boss.
A touch of madness!

Unless you cut the string,
you'll never really live.

Zorba
(a free translation)

DO NOT DISTURB!

All of us shrink from
searching honestly
for a deeper meaning to life.

The attitude "who says so" or
"why bother"
is not always a sign of
closed-mindedness
or lack of interest.
It may be a symptom of
deep-down fear.

We fear the unknown.
We seek security: four walls,
a ceiling, and a floor.
Perhaps we don't want to
"risk" the consequences of
thinking deeply.
It might disturb our cozy world.

Is this why
people sometimes bend their belief
to their life style,
rather than shape their life style
to their belief?

CAUTION

Doubt is almost
a natural phase of life;
but
as certainly as it is natural,
it is also temporary,

unless
it is unwisely
wrought into conduct.

Theodore Munger

ASK YOURSELF

Wonder about
your basic state of mind and soul,
how certain or uncertain you are,
how happy or unhappy,

whether you live in
a state of inner assurance,
a state of doubt,
a state of quiet desperation . . .

Ask yourself ultimately
about your image of God,
what God was to you,
what he is to you now,
what you expect of him.

John S. Dunne
A Search for God in Time and Memory

INVITATION

To move,
on the level of feelings,
from the reality of experience
to that of faith
can be terrifying and bewildering.

But it is
in this very movement toward faith
that persons are called upon
to affirm their trust and joy
in being part of something greater
than themselves.

Diane Plummer

AWAKENING

To discover God
is not to discover an idea
but to discover oneself.
It is to awaken
to that part of one's existence
which has been hidden from sight
and which one has refused to recognize.

The discovery may be very painful;
it is like going through
a kind of death.

But it is the one thing
which makes life
worth living.

Bede Griffith
The Golden String

OR

The greatest sin
is
not to care,
or
not
to make the effort.

GROWTH POWER

Human knowledge grows through
faith, reason, and experience.
And the greatest contributor to growth
is faith.

Sometimes we discover new insights
on our own.
But usually what we discover
is intertwined with faith.

We know the shape of the United States
and the location
of its valleys, rivers, and mountains,
because we have maps.

How do we know
that the maps are accurate?
Actually, we don't;
we have faith in map makers.

Maps are the product of
the combined effort of many surveyors.
Maps are known to be accurate
only by the teams that surveyed them.

The accuracy of the whole
is a matter of faith.

FAITH IS . . .

To believe only possibilities
is not faith,
but mere philosophy.

Thomas Browne

TWO MEANINGS

I may have faith
that a certain horse
will win the Kentucky Derby.
I may believe it so strongly
that I will bet on the horse.

In this case, my "belief"
is a matter of probability
or subjective opinion.

But the word "belief" or "faith"
has a far different meaning.
It has nothing to do with
probability or opinion.

If the girl I am about to marry
tells me,
"I love you!"
I really believe her.
I do not question it.

In this case my "belief"/"faith"
is a matter of certitude, not probability.
I am certain
because I love her
and she loves me.

Faith is
not a formula
which is agreed to
if the weight of evidence
favors it.

Walter Lippman

Faith is
reaching out to Love
in love.

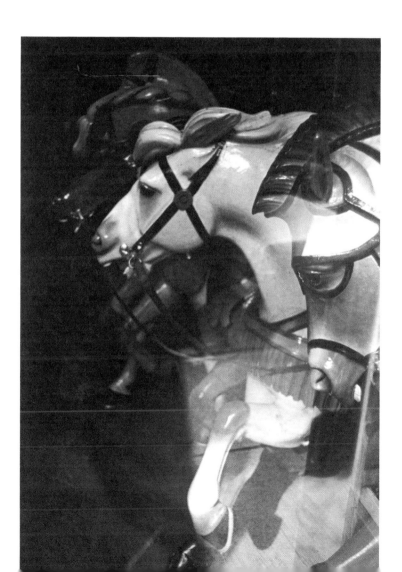

"I BELIEVE"

I still believe that people
are really good at heart . . .
If I look into the heavens
I think that it will all come out right,
and that peace and tranquility
will return again.

Anne Frank

UP TO YOU

Faith is, after all,
an admixture
of light and darkness.

We will always have
enough darkness with us
to justify the refusal of light.

But we will always have
enough light to allow us
to bear the darkness.

Louis Evely
The Gospels Without Myth

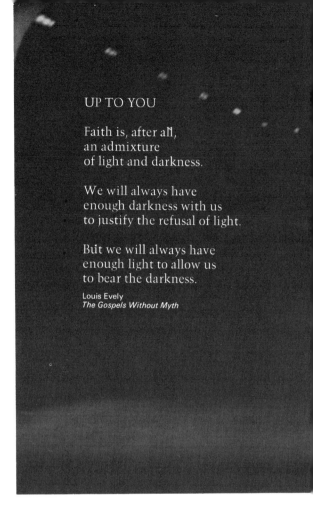

Thirteen-year-old Anne
wrote this in her diary
while she and her parents
were hiding from the Nazis
in World War II.

Was Anne's faith
in the goodness of people
merely an opinion?
Or was it rooted in
something
deeper than mere logic?

Anne expressed
this belief
in the face of horrifying events
that drove other men
to despair. Why?

DEATH AND BIRTH

The courage to be
is rooted in
the God who appears

when God
has disappeared
in the anxiety of doubt.

Paul Tillich

CRY
IN THE NIGHT

Lord,
I do believe.

Help me
believe more.

Mark 9:24

FLIGHT FROM FEAR

My Lord God,
I have no idea where I am going.
I do not see the road ahead of me.
I cannot know for certain
where it will end.
Nor do I really know myself,

and the fact that
I think that I am following your will
does not mean
that I am actually doing so.

But I believe
that the desire to please you
does in fact please you.

And I hope that I
have that desire in all that I am doing.
I hope that I will never do anything
apart from that desire.
And I know that if I do this
you will lead me by the right road
though I may know nothing about it.

Therefore will I trust you always
though I may seem to be lost
and in the shadow of death.

I will not fear,
for you are ever with me,
and you will never
leave me to face my perils alone.

Thomas Merton

89

YOU WILL KNOW

How long must I wait?
God knows.
He can give himself to you overnight,
you can also wait twenty years . . .

One day he will come.
Once in the stillness . . .
you will know . . .

Not from a book
or the word of someone else,
but through him.

Romano Guardini
The Lord

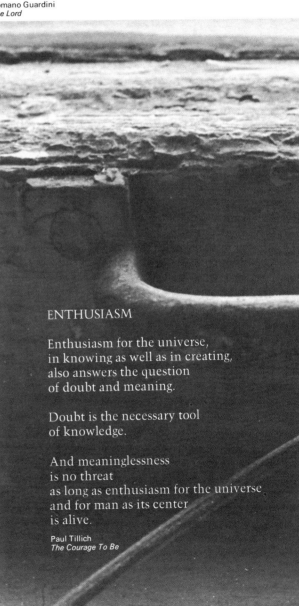

NO THUNDER

Entering
the
forest

he
moves
not
the
grass;

Entering
the
water

he
makes
not
a
ripple.

The Zenrin

ENTHUSIASM

Enthusiasm for the universe,
in knowing as well as in creating,
also answers the question
of doubt and meaning.

Doubt is the necessary tool
of knowledge.

And meaninglessness
is no threat
as long as enthusiasm for the universe
and for man as its center
is alive.

Paul Tillich
The Courage To Be

PEOPLE WHO SHOUT DOUBT

For the Word
    for the Word was at the birth
    of the beginning.
It made the Heavens and the Earth
    and set them spinning,
And for several million years
It's withstood all our forums
    and bad ideas . . .

There are people who doubt it,
There are people who doubt it
    and shout it out loud.
There are local vocal yokels
    who we know collect a crowd.
They can fashion a rebuttal
    that's as subtle as a sword,
But they're never gonna scuttle
    the Word of the Lord.

Leonard Bernstein
Stephen Schwartz
for *Mass*

SUN RISE

My
hosanna
has
come
forth

from
the
crucible
of
doubt.

Feodor Dostoevski

MORNING JOY

There may be tears
during the night,

but joy comes
in the morning.

Psalm 30:5

THE MIRACLE

Tight as a headache
the congested crags
hem in the traveler

but suddenly
the humped obsession
cracks
and clapping waves
cry alleluia.

With
my fingers cupped
I kneel again
by the forgotten lake,
lifting infinity.

Sydney Carter
Nothing Fixed or Final

6

NO "SEEING" QUITE THE SAME AGAIN

new consciousness

NO "SEEING"
IS QUITE THE SAME AGAIN

Helen Keller, who was
born blind, deaf, and dumb,
writes about this incident
with her teacher:

She brought me my hat,
and I knew I was going out
into the warm sunshine.
This thought,
if a wordless sensation
may be called a thought,
made me hop and skip with pleasure.

We walked down the path
to the well-house,
attracted by the fragrance of the
honeysuckle with which it was covered.
Someone was drawing water
and my teacher placed my hand
under the spout.

As the cool stream
gushed over my hand
she spelled into the other the word *water*,
first slowly, then rapidly.
I stood still, my whole attention fixed
upon the motion of her fingers.

Suddenly I felt a misty consciousness
as of something forgotten—
a thrill of returning thought;
and somehow the mystery of language
was revealed to me.
I knew then that w-a-t-e-r meant
the wonderful cool something that
was flowing over my hand.

That living word awakened my soul,
gave it light, hope, joy,
set it free!
There were barriers still, it is true,
but barriers
that in time could be swept away.

I left the well-house eager to learn.
Everything had a name,
and each name gave birth
to a new thought.

As we returned to the house
every object which I touched
seemed to quiver with life.
That was because
I saw everything with the strange,
new sight that had come to me.

Helen Keller
The Story of My Life

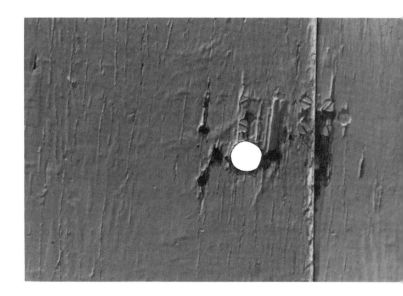

NEW VISION

[Faith] transforms man,
it relates him in a new way
to the whole of reality
and therefore creates
a new human self-consciousness.

Gregory Baum
Faith And Doctrine

PROFOUND CHANGE

The closest human model
for the understanding of divine faith
is the effect
which certain human encounters
have on us.

Having met this remarkable person,
having listened to him
and believed him,
my life has been profoundly changed:

I understand myself in a new way;
I experience the world in a different light.

Gregory Baum
Faith And Doctrine

REVOLUTION

The life of faith
demands a revolution
in our sense of reality.

In our consciousness . . .
the body is
more real than the soul;
electricity
more real than thought;
power
more real than love;
utility
more real than truth.
Together they form the world—
incomparably more real
than God.

How difficult . . .
even in prayer
to sense the reality of God . . .
to mix with people,
perform the duties of the day . .
and still to say,
God is more real
than all this . . .

Romano Guardini
The Lord

NEW LIFE

A man's mind,
stretched by a new idea,
can never go back
to its original dimension.

Oliver Wendell Holmes

BIBLICAL IDEA OF GOD

For Israel
God was the beginning,
God was the end.
God was above, God was below.
God was all.

God was at the heart
of Israel's life.
All reality
was rooted in
and oriented toward God.

Above all,
God was a God of human concern,
a God who wanted to save man.

God's concern for man
is reflected in
the biblical image
of God as "Father."

I AM ME!

Believing that God is Father
changes the way we experience life.
We acquire a new awareness
of ourselves and
of our relationship to . . . reality . . .

To believe that God is Father
initiates me into a new consciousness
of myself as son . . .
I have a destiny.
I do not have to create this destiny . . .
This destiny makes me someone . . .
I rejoice in myself.

To believe that God is Father
means to believe
that men are destined to be brothers, and
that salvation is at work in their history.

God revealing himself as Father discloses . . .
a new self-awareness—
"I am son"—
a new experience of the world—
"We are a family."

Gregory Baum
Faith And Doctrine

CLOSER

. . . the atheist who believes in man
and scorns God
can be closer to holiness
than the religionist
who believes in God
and scorns man.

Sydney J. Harris

If someone says,
"I love God,"
yet hates his brother,
he is a liar.

For he cannot love God,
whom he has not seen,
if he does not love his brother,
whom he has seen.

I John 4:20

GOD OF CONCERN

The Israelite
had a sharp sense of being part
of a community.

He lived in a tribe.
His name was a tribal name,
and his work was a tribal activity.
He was measured as an individual
in terms of his tribal contribution.

He saw his fulfillment and destiny
inseparably bound up with
the whole of Israel.

This community consciousness
permeates not only the 45 books
of the Old Testament,
but also the 27 books
of the New Testament.
The Israelite
experienced Yahweh as a social God,
deeply concerned about all men.

THERE
I STAND

Wherever
you
see

the
trace
of
man

there
I
stand
before
you.

A rabbinical
interpretation

BETTER NAKED

Who can separate
his faith from his actions,
or his belief from his occupation?

Who can spread
his hours before him, saying:
"This for God and
this for myself . . ."

He who wears his morality
but as his best garment
were better naked.

Kahlil Gibran
The Prophet

FOR LISTENERS ONLY

There is much in us
that is afraid of truth . . .
We have positions to defend
and privileges to cling to . . .

If divine revelation
makes me a listener I am able to
leave the confines of my own wisdom,
listen to the message present
in my daily experiences and be . . .
open to the summons that creates
new life . . .

Believing that God is Word
creates a new relationship to other people
since it means acknowledging that
the mystery of death and resurrection
alive in oneself also addresses other men.
It creates a new . . . orientation to the world
as a family of men,
summoned to growth and reconciliation . . .

Gregory Baum
Faith And Doctrine

LISTEN

The more faithfully
you listen
to the voice within you,

the better
you will hear
what is sounding outside.

Dag Hammarskjöld
Markings

If you hear the music,
join the dancing.

LOOK AROUND

Once, as she was being led
to her waiting car, Helen Keller
paused and gazed lovingly at the sky.
With her sightless eyes,
she seemed to be watching
the great masses of white clouds
press toward the horizon.

Finally, she gave a deep sigh,
then allowed her companion
to help her into the car.

As it pulled away,
Helen Keller said aloud:
"The greatest calamity that could
befall a person, is to have sight
and fail to see."

John Vitale
"Beauty is Everywhere"

LIGHT OR DARKNESS

The eyes are like
a lamp for the body:

if your eyes are clear,
your whole body
will be full of light;

but if your eyes are bad,
your whole body
will be in darkness.

Matthew 6:22–23

TOMORROW
WILL BE DIFFERENT

God is not only "Father,"
who gives identity and destiny.
He is not only "Word,"
who calls to new life.
He is also "Spirit,"
who empowers us to become
more fully human.

"There is an inexhaustible creativity
alive in men, and in others, so that
tomorrow will be different from today.
Man is not trapped in the world:
God as Spirit is at work in men
producing the new creation . . .

We are alive,
and other people are alive
thanks to a mystery that takes place
at the core of our being . . .
giving courage,
producing growth,
making us capable of love . . .
creating insight,
calling life out of death.

Faith evokes in men the new consciousness
that they are alive
with a life that triumphs over death."

Gregory Baum
Faith And Doctrine

GOD'S GLORY

The glory of God
is man fully alive.

St. Irenaeus

IN TOUCH

God is
the transcendent mystery
at the core
of human history,
the deepest dimension
of human life . . .
who calls us . . .
and graces us . . .
to become more fully human . . .

The inner gesture
of prayer therefore [is] . . .
the attempt to be . . .
more reflectively present
to what happens every day . . .
an attempt to be in touch with
the root of one's personal existence
and the mystery alive
in the community.

Gregory Baum
"Are We Losing the Faith?"

7

TAKE OFF
YOUR SHOES

rediscovery of wonder

HOLY GROUND

Meanwhile Moses . . .
was surprised to see that the bush,
though on fire, was not consumed.
So Moses decided,
"I must go over to look at
this remarkable sight,
and see why the bush is not burned."

When the Lord saw him coming over
to look at it more closely,
God called out to him from the bush,
"Moses! Moses!"

He answered, "Here I am."

God said, "Come no nearer!
Remove the sandals from your feet,
for the place where you stand
is holy ground.
I am the God of your father . . ."

Exodus 3:1–6

FOLLOW

Come ride the wind
when it blows
and follow,
follow to where
it goes.

NO TIME

Contemplation is a casualty
of the American way of life.
We simply do not have time for it.

We read poetry
as we would a detective story . . .
We visit art museums
as we would tour the Grand Canyon.

Andrew Greeley
The Critic

AFIRE

Earth's
crammed
with
heaven,

And
every
common
bush
afire
with
God;

And
only
he
who
sees

takes
off
his
shoes

The
rest
sit
round
it

and
pluck
blackberries.

E. B. Browning

SMALL WONDER

In the global village wrought by TV
both the marvelous and the appalling
quickly become commonplace.

Men walk on the moon.
The dream of centuries realized.
Yet after viewing
the first moon walk live for only a short time,
millions found the event tedious
and went to bed.

Atrocities, burnings and deaths
are brought into your living room daily . . .
Who can feel outrage every single evening?
Who can help but eventually be bored?

Small wonder, then,
that you've lost touch with the simple delights
of a minute perception—
such as becoming aware of air
against your face,
or observing the subtle ballet of grass in a breeze,
or savoring fully the aromas of spring.

Howard R. Lewis and
Harold S. Streitfeld
Growth Games

THE SOURCE

. . . we die on the day
when our lives cease to be illumined
by the steady radiance
renewed daily,

of a wonder,
the source of which
is beyond reason.

Dag Hammarskjöld
Markings

THE GARDEN

We are stardust,
we are golden—

and we've got to get ourselves
back to the garden.

Joni Mitchell

A SEINE

When I'm playful
I use the meridians of longitude
and parallels of latitude
for a seine,
and drag the Atlantic Ocean
for whales!

Mark Twain
Life on the Mississippi

NEW FRONTIER

The greatest unexplored area
lies under your hat.

Author unknown

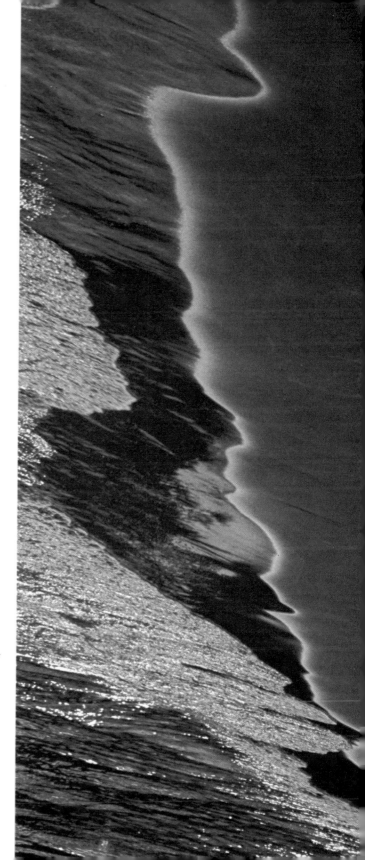

WHAT IS SO IMPORTANT
ABOUT NOON?

One blustery weekend
I was strolling with my little boy
on an Atlantic beach.
We were sailing clamshells into the onshore wind
and watching them curve back to us.
I don't know why this was fun.
But on that morning sailing clamshells
seemed like the best of all possible things to do.

After a while I looked at my watch.
It was lunchtime.
We left the beach reluctantly.

Only after we sat down to eat did I wonder
why I had stopped that game.
What is so important about noon?
Why must we be hypnotized by the clock?
My boy and I went back to the beach after lunch
but the mood was gone.
The clamshells and the wind did nothing for us now
but blow sand in our eyes.

Max Gunther
The Weekenders

A BEGINNING

To be surprised, to wonder,
is to begin to understand.

Jose Ortega y Gasset

ALICE

After falling down the rabbit hole,
Alice eventually comes to a long, low hall.
On the table she finds
a bottle marked "Drink Me!"

Alice drinks and soon finds herself
shutting up like a telescope.
This made her a little nervous
for, as she said to herself,

"It might end, you know . . .
in my going out altogether like a candle.
I wonder what I should be like then?"
And she tried to fancy what
the flame of a candle looks like
after the candle is blown out,
for she could not remember
ever having seen such a thing.

Lewis Carroll
Alice's Adventures in Wonderland

SHOULDN'T WE?

Like the "father on the beach"
and like Alice
shouldn't we take time off
to wonder about the mystery
of life?

Shouldn't we ponder what it means
when we realize that
the earth upon which we walk
dates back 4,500 million years;
that vegetation, blanketing our hills
goes back over 400 million years;
that animals, co-habiting our planet,
arch back 350 million years;
we ourselves emerged
only within the last one million years?

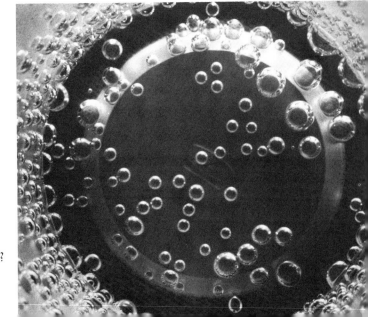

SEA WONDER

The oceans that cool man's earth
are also adventures in wonder.

The sea floors are carpeted
with mountains as tall as Mt. Everest,
and are sculptured with gorges
that run deeper than the Grand Canyon.

20,000 species of fish
are but a fraction of
the sea's unmet population.

CHANCE GIFTS

Rollers on the beach, wind in the pines,
the slow flapping of herons across sand dunes,
drown out the hectic rhythms
of time tables and schedules.
One falls under their spells,
relaxes, stretches out prone.

One becomes, in fact,
like the element on which one lies,
flattened by the sea;
bare, open, empty as the beach,
erased by today's tides
of all yesterday's scribblings.

And then,
some morning in the second week,
the mind wakes, comes to life again . . .
It begins to drift, to play,
to turn over in gentle careless rolls
like those lazy waves on the beach.
One never knows what chance treasures
these easy unconscious rollers may toss up
on the smooth white sand
of the conscious mind . . .

Anne Morrow Lindbergh
Gift From The Sea

A MATTER OF FACT

Far away
in some strange constellation
in the skies . . .
there is a star
which astronomers
may some day discover . . .
though as a matter of fact
they were walking about on it
all of the time.

Gilbert K. Chesterton
The Everlasting Man

Do not let your hearts be troubled.
Have faith in God
and faith in me.
In my Father's house there are many
    dwelling places.

John 14:1–2

EXQUISITE BLENDING

A part of the human ear
is a series of some four thousand
minute but complex arches
graduated with exquisite regularity
in size and shape . . .
and transmit in some manner to the brain,
every cadence of sound or voice,
from the thunderclap to the whisper of pines
and the exquisite blending of the tones
and harmonies of every instrument in
the orchestra.

A. Cressy Morrison
Man Does Not Stand Alone

BLIND

I have walked with people
whose eyes are full of light
but who see nothing in sea or sky,
nothing in city streets,
nothing in books.

It were far better to sail forever
in the night of blindness . . .
than to be content
with the mere act of seeing.

The only lightless dark
is the night of darkness
in ignorance and insensibility.

Helen Keller

ONLY A BOY

I do not know
what I may appear to the world,
but to myself
I seem to have been only a boy
playing on the seashore,
and diverting myself
in now and then finding a smoother pebble .
whilst the great ocean of truth
lay all undiscovered before me.

Isaac Newton

UNWRAP THE GIFTS

The gloom of the world
is but a shadow.
Behind it, yet within reach,
is joy.
There is radiance and glory
in the darkness,
could we but see,
and to see,
we have only to look.
I beseech you to look.

Life is so generous a giver,
but we,
judging its gifts by their covering,
cast them away as ugly,
or heavy, or hard.
Remove the covering,
and you will find beneath it
a living splendor,
woven of love,
by wisdom,
with power . . .

Everything we call a trial,
a sorrow or a duty,
believe me . . .
the gift is there,
and the wonder
of an overshadowing presence.
Our joys too:
be not content with them
as joys.
They, too conceal diviner gifts.

Fra Giovanni
1513 A.D.

SKY WONDER

Above the sea world is the sky world.
More than 8,000 known and named species of birds
wing windward over hills and
through cloud banks.
Migratory birds navigate with pinpoint accuracy.
Some suggest that they use
the sun and stars as compass points.
Take the Manx Shearwater.

One of these birds
was caught and marked in Wales.
It was then flown over 3 thousand miles
to Boston where it was released.
Within two weeks, the Manx Shearwater was
back in Wales at the very spot
where it was captured.

SIGHTLESS

The man
who cannot wonder
is but a pair of spectacles
behind which
there is no eyes.

Thomas Carlyle

VAGABOUND ARTIST

Scattering a thousand graces,
he passed through these groves in haste,
and looking upon them as he went,
left them by his glance alone,
clothed with beauty.

St. John of the Cross

SPACE WONDER

Beyond the playground of the birds
lies the moon—on whose powdered surface
man has walked.

Beyond the moon arches a canopy
of endless stars and star-families.
All of these orbiting bodies
are fellow space travelers
moving silently through the vast chasm
of the seemingly endless expanse of universe.
They form families of suns, all children,
apparently, of a common birth.

WHERE?

Where could I go
to escape from your Spirit?
Where could I get away from
your presence?
If I went up to heaven,
you would be there . . .
If I flew away beyond the east
or lived in the
farthest place in the west,
you would be there to lead me,
you would be there
to help me.

Psalm 139:7-10

BY MYSELF

When the proofs, the figures,
    were ranged in columns before me . . .
How soon
    unaccountably I became tired and sick.
Till rising and gliding out
    I wander'd off by myself,
In the mystical moist night-air,
    and from time to time,
Look'd up in perfect silence at the stars.

Walt Whitman
"When I Heard The
Learn'd Astronomer"

113

FROM AARDVARK TO . . .

Nature is
a collage of millions of billions
of parts
perfectly interwoven
and intricately functioning
with unbelievable precision
and unity.

WHAT IS MAN?

When I look at the sky,
which you have made,
at the moon and the stars,
which you set in their places—

what is man,
that you think of him;
mere man, that you care for him?

Psalm 8:2-3

EXPERIMENT

Take ten pennies
and mark them 1 to 10.
Put them in your pocket
and give them a good shake.
Now try to draw them out in sequence
from 1 to 10, putting each coin back
in your pocket after each draw.

Your chances of drawing 1 is 1 in 10.
Your chances of drawing 1 and 2
in succession would be 1 in 100.
Your chances of drawing 1-3
in succession would be 1 in 1,000.
This would continue
until your chances of drawing 1 to 10
in succession would skyrocket
to the unbelievable figure of
1 in 10 billion.

adapted from
A. Cressy Morrison
Man Does Not Stand Alone

TIMELINE

4,500 million years ago the earth was formed.
Just for fun
let's collapse the time scale a millionfold.

"This means that a year ago
the first man learned to use
certain odd-shaped sticks and stones
as tools and weapons.
Speech appeared.

Then, only last week
someone developed the art of
skillfully shaping stones to meet his needs.

Day before yesterday
man was sufficiently an artist to use
simplified pictures as symbolic writing.
Yesterday the alphabet was introduced . . .

Last midnight Rome fell . . .
Galileo observed his falling bodies at 8:15
this morning . . .
At 11:40 X-rays were discovered by Roentgen,
followed quickly by radium and wireless telegraphy.

Only 15 minutes ago the automobile
came into general use . . .
And not until a minute ago have we had
worldwide broadcasts by short-wave radio."

Arthur H. Compton
Science magazine

NO WAY BACK

Lean on the future. There
if anywhere
you walk upon the water.

All that was true at first
is true at last
but there is no way back
into the past

But through the future. There
is anywhere
the miracle must happen.

Sydney Carter
Nothing Fixed or Final

BEYOND DREAMS

And scarce do we guess
the things of earth,

and what is within our grasp
we find with difficulty;

but when the things are of heaven,
who can search them out?

Wisdom 9:16

BREAKTHROUGH

Someday,
after mastering
the winds, the waves,
the tides and gravity,
we shall harness for God
the energies of love,

and then,
for the second time
in the history of the world,
man will discover fire.

Teilhard de Chardin

TRANSFORMATION ONLY

Science . . . tells us
that nothing in nature,
not even the tiniest particle,
can disappear without a trace.
Nature does not know extinction.
All it knows is transformation . . .

And everything science
has taught me . . .
strengthens my belief
in the continuity of our
spiritual existence after death.
Nothing disappears without a trace.

Wernher von Braun
This Week Magazine

THE GOOD NEWS

Men of Athens . . .
as I walked through your city
and looked at the places
where you worship,
I found . . .
an altar on which is written,

"To an Unknown God."

That which you worship . . .
even though you do not know it,
is what I now proclaim to you.

God who made the world
and everything in it,
is Lord of heaven and earth,
and does not live in temples
made by men . . .

It is he himself
who gives life and breath and
everything else to men . . .

"In him we live and move and are."

Acts 17:22-25, 28

BEYOND WONDER

If seeds
in the black earth can turn
into beautiful roses,

what might not
the heart of man become
in its long journey to the stars?

Gilbert K. Chesterton

WONDER/WORSHIP

Wonder
is the basis
of worship.

Thomas Carlyle

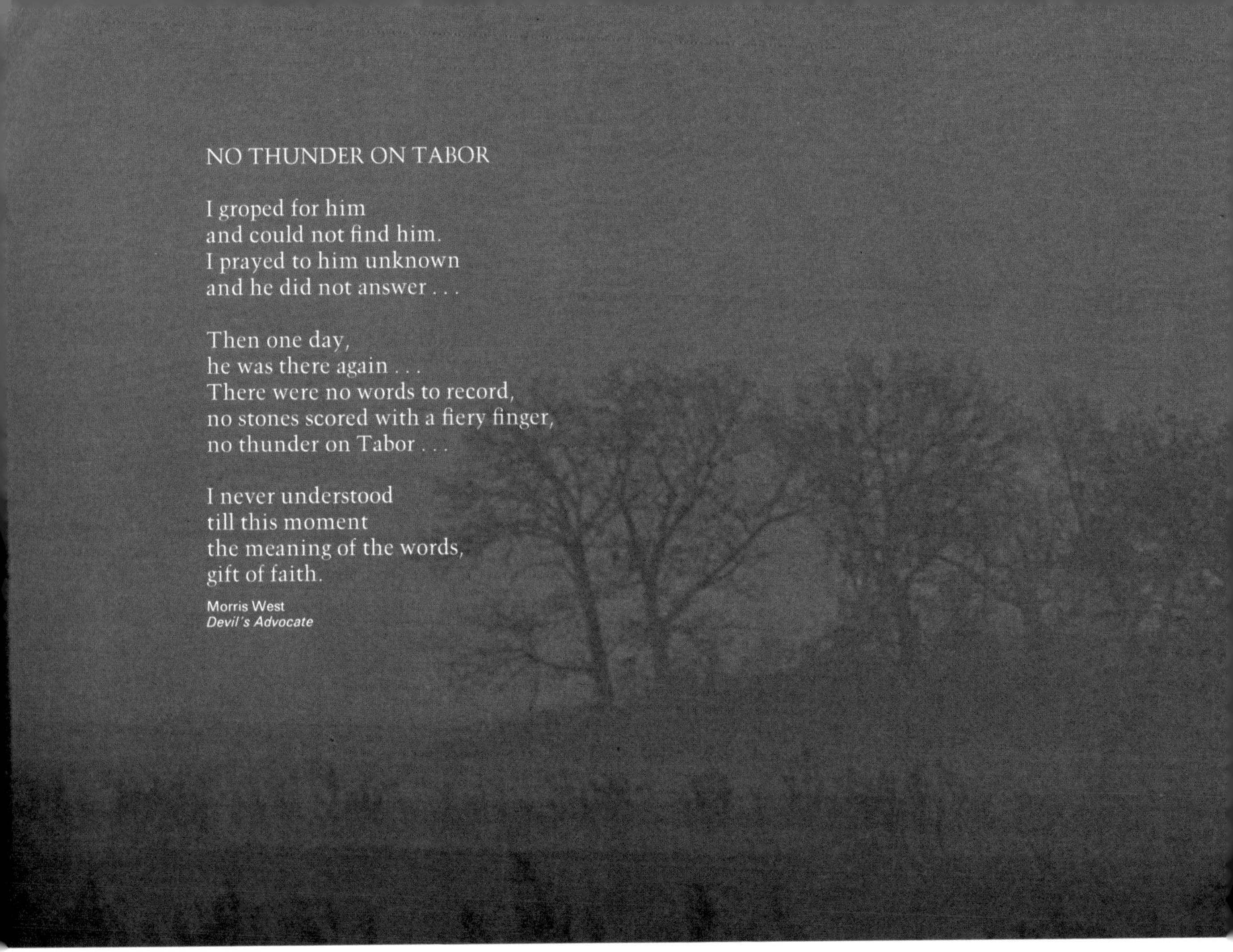

NO THUNDER ON TABOR

I groped for him
and could not find him.
I prayed to him unknown
and he did not answer . . .

Then one day,
he was there again . . .
There were no words to record,
no stones scored with a fiery finger,
no thunder on Tabor . . .

I never understood
till this moment
the meaning of the words,
gift of faith.

Morris West
Devil's Advocate

118

ALL THINGS NEW

Then I saw new heavens
and a new earth.
The former heavens and
the former earth had passed away,
and the sea was no longer.

I also saw a new Jerusalem,
the holy city,
coming out of heaven from God,
beautiful as a bride
prepared to meet her husband.

I heard a loud voice
from the throne cry out:
"This is God's dwelling among men.

He shall dwell with them
and they shall be his people
and he shall be their God
who is always with them.

He shall wipe every tear
from their eyes,
and there shall be no more
death or mourning,
crying out or pain,
for the former world
has passed away.

See, I make all things new!"

Book of Revelations 21:1-5

Jesus said to Phillip, "Whoever has seen me has seen the Father... I am in the Father and the Father is in me."

JOHN 14:9